THE CROSS APPLIED
Finding Life in Jesus' Death

Testimonials

"This study came at a time in my life when I have been going through some very deep struggles. The course has been so relevant to my life. Each day through the lessons, God provided the encouragement and support I needed and gave me the right things to share with family members who needed insight and encouragement. I've been a believer for over thirty years, but this study has brought me closer to Christ than I have ever been. I wish every believer would take it; I genuinely believe that it would have a major impact on the church to examine the cross of Christ in such depth. And I wish every non-believer would take it—how could they then not give their hearts and lives to Jesus Christ?" —**Debbie**

"When I first thought about doing a 30 lesson Bible study about the cross, I wondered how that was possible. This study has caused me to want to spend the rest of my life studying, meditating on, and rejoicing in all that Jesus accomplished there. I love Jesus more than I ever have, and God has really re-kindled my desire to tell others about him." —**Jerry**

"These have been the most helpful study I have ever experienced. I have not only gained useful and insightful knowledge, but my relationship with Jesus has grown better, and I feel I am better able to worship Him and live the life that He wants me to live, now that I have seen the great lengths that He went through to save me from eternal damnation. I can see much better the gift He gave to mankind. Jesus' death on the cross is typically treated as a kind of "Christianity 101;" once one has learned of it, they move on to more "important" things but, as the Cross study has shown me, Jesus' death and resurrection is the epicenter of our faith; it is the beginning and the end of all things." —**William**

"I have completed the Cross study and find myself incredibly blessed and enlightened every day. I can also attest that it has strengthened my faith and my walk with Christ. I am recommending it to everyone. I am even thinking about how to do the study with men at my church. It is THAT good and THAT valuable. I think it helps us have a better understanding of the awesome gift that God has given us in and through His son Jesus Christ." —*Glenn*

"For many years, I was held captive by the devil and, over time, he dragged me deeper and deeper into worse sin and self-abuse. I eventually gave up my business and my friends and became a hermit. When my wife left, I knew I was dying inside; I was miserable all the time and wanted to be left alone with my sin. The day came when I thought about taking my own life, and I decided to seek help from God. My spouse sent me an email about a ministry called Setting Captives Free. I thought that it would be just a dumb class but, by the end of the sixty days, I was free of my sin and God had taken me under His wing. He taught me how to fight and supplied the arsenal of weapons. I needed to know more, so I did the Cross study. I am totally overwhelmed by this study, in a good way. I never knew the many reasons why Jesus was sacrificed by his Father for us. I am happy to say that my spouse and I are again best friends, attend Sunday services, and pray together. Thank you, Jesus and your Father, the Almighty God." —*Robert*

setting CAPTIVES free

THE CROSS APPLIED

— Finding Life in Jesus' Death —

MIKE CLEVELAND

SETTING CAPTIVES FREE
PUBLISHING

Setting Captives Free Publishing
1400 W. Washington St., Ste. 104
Sequim, WA 98382

ISBN: 978-1-7337609-6-6
LCCN: 2020911720

I joyfully dedicate this book to my dear brother,
Petrus Zijlstra.

Petrus has devoted his life to living and teaching the
gospel of Jesus Christ. As an elder in his church, Petrus gives of his
time, wisdom, and cross-focused counsel in his church. As a volunteer
mentor and Board Member for Setting Captives Free, Petrus has provided
nearly two decades of counsel to us, along with consistent cross-focused
encouragement to many people all over the world.

Petrus, your hours of translation work, mentoring, and supervising
are greatly appreciated, but even more, your passion and encouragement to look to
Jesus in all things! Faithfully, you have invited me (and many others) to look
to the cross of Jesus to see the love, justice, righteousness, and holiness of
God so that our hearts would be cut and healed by the wounds of Jesus,
and we would experience His resurrection power.

Petrus, thank you for always pointing me to the cross,
both in your life and in your words.
You are dearly loved!

Table of Contents

Introduction

*D*estructive teaching has come into the church in the past century, teaching that essentially says: "the gospel is the 'salvation message.' It is for unbelievers to 'get saved, and then we move on to deeper teachings.'" The implication is that the gospel is a spiritual kindergarten through which we pass, tipping our hats to the cross, on our way to the deeper teachings of the Bible. This teaching is destructive because it insinuates that once we believe the gospel, we are good to go, we can move beyond it to more significant things.

But this teaching of 'receive the gospel and then move on' is a half-truth. The gospel is indeed the salvation message; it is "the power of God unto salvation" (Romans 1:16). But it is also a sanctification message, in other words, that which sets believers apart from our sins.

In Galatians 3, Paul wrote to believers who were trying to set themselves apart from sin by their efforts at keeping the Law, and what he says to them in verse 1 is startling. He says, *"you foolish Galatians, who has bewitched you? Before your very eyes, Jesus Christ was clearly portrayed as crucified."* In other words, Paul preached the cross of Christ as the message that not only saves from sin but also separates from sin. The cross is not merely a salvation message; it is also a sanctification message.

The message of the cross is the power of God *for believers*, as stated here:

> *"The message of the cross is foolish to those who are headed for destruction! But **we who are being saved know it is the very power of God.** [19] As the Scriptures say, "I will destroy the wisdom of the wise and discard the intelligence of the intelligent." 1 Corinthians 1:18-19 (NLT)*

The message of the cross is foolish to those who are headed for destruction! But we who are being saved know it is the very power of God.

But it is not only a salvation message, it is not only a sanctification message; it is also a stabilization message.

> "Now to him who is able to establish you (strengthen, confirm, stabilize you) by my gospel and the preaching of Jesus Christ, according to the revelation of the mystery hidden for long ages past," Romans 16:25

Do you want to know how to become stabilized in life, how to have a firm foundation, how to become rooted and grounded, how to be constant and steady and firmly planted, unshakeable? Paul says it is *by my gospel and the preaching of Jesus Christ.*

This study was written for anyone who wishes to look at the many aspects of the cross of Jesus Christ as it applies not only to salvation but also to our daily walk. It seeks to *not* be a shallow portrayal of the unfathomable riches of Christ, but rather to dig deep into the meaning, and reveal the *divine power* of the cross of Jesus Christ.

It was also written for those who do not believe, or for any who wish to understand the distinctive difference between Christianity and every religion. Say to any Muslim, Hindu, or Buddhist, "Fear God, hate sin, repent" and he will agree with you. Only the Christian message tells of a Substitute who died in our place to save us from our sins. Only the Christian faith declares that we gain heaven not by our works but by the life and death of another, Jesus Christ, Who purchased our eternal life when He died in our place and rose from the dead.

Finally, this study is written to show the many places that the Old Testament reveals the gospel of Jesus Christ. The gospel tells us that Christ died for our sins, "according to the Scriptures," that He was buried, that He was raised on the third day "according to the Scriptures" (1 Corinthians 15:3-5), and so our purpose in this book is to see the gospel in the Old Testament Scriptures. This kind of study can produce unexpected joy and delight as we are surprised, time and time again, at places where we may have not seen the gospel previously.

"*The gospel begins, not in Matthew 1:1, but in Genesis. Let us never forget that, and so let us go to our Old Testament and look for the gospel. You will find it there almost everywhere in a most astounding manner, and it is our business, as well as our privilege, to seek it and to rejoice in it as we find it there.*

...the Bible teaches very clearly that there is only one gospel; the gospel is the same in the Old Testament as it is in the New. Again, I am surprised when a preacher does not see it in the Old Testament, for if a man does not see it there, I doubt if he understands the gospel in the New Testament. Take the gospel that was preached by God in the Garden of Eden and also the promise made to Abraham; that is the essence of the gospel. Look at all the types and shadows, look at the various offerings described in Leviticus and elsewhere. Look even at the very furniture of the tabernacle. All these things preach the gospel; they are the types of the gospel and its message."— Dr. Martyn Lloyd-Jones"[1]

---

[1]   Lloyd-Jones, Martyn, *Great Doctrines of the Bible (Three Volumes in One): God the Father, God the Son; God the Holy Spirit; The Church and the Last Things* (Wheaton, IL: Crossway, 2003). https://www.monergism.com/covenant-grace-old-testament

The Reason for our Study

*M*aybe you are wondering, why all the fuss about the cross? What can we possibly discover at the cross that would warrant a whole book? In this lesson, we are going to introduce our study, and consider just how significant the death of Jesus Christ is.

Can you imagine a subject so important that somebody would determine to know only it and nothing else? Is there any specific subject in your life that is so important that you have decided that it would be the main subject of your entire life, that you would seek to have your life revolve around it and direct all your conversations toward it?

Paul had one such subject. Let's see what it was:

> *"And I, when I came to you, brothers, did not come proclaiming to you the testimony of God with lofty speech or wisdom.[2] I decided to know nothing among you except Jesus Christ and him crucified.[3] And I was with you in weakness and in fear and much trembling,[4] my speech and my message were not in plausible words of wisdom, but in demonstration of the Spirit and of power,[5] that your faith might not rest in the wisdom of men but in the power of God." 1 Corinthians 2:1-5*

Question 1. According to 1 Corinthians 2:1-2, what was Paul's message to the Corinthians?

_____

_____

_____

_____

Next, please review Romans 1:16 to give additional perspective:

> *"For I am not ashamed of the gospel, for it is the power of God for salvation to everyone who believes, to the Jew first and also to the Greek." Romans 1:16*

Question 2. According to Romans 1:16 and 1 Corinthians 2:1-5, what is the gospel (the death and resurrection of Jesus Christ) called?

_____

_____

_____

_____

We note that the death of Jesus Christ was Paul's one subject, which was of such importance that he decided to know nothing but the cross. Wow! That is some kind of focus, isn't it? That is certainly being single-minded. And we also notice that in Romans 1:16 Paul called the gospel of Jesus Christ (His death and resurrection) *"the power of God"*, and in 1 Corinthians 2:1-5 he set this *"power of God"* in opposition to *"the wisdom of man."*

When we examine the cross in all its splendor, and we experience the power of God in it, we, too, find that it is all-consuming in its attraction to us. The cross first convicts us of sin, as we see God's hatred for it. We may minimize sin, excuse it away, and shift blame to others, but all this must stop as we view the cross. Then the cross draws sinners who know they are guilty, whose consciences now trouble them greatly, who fear the wrath of God, to come and receive forgiveness of their sins, find freedom from their sins, and enjoy a whole new life in Jesus Christ.

"Now is the judgment of this world; now will the ruler of this world be cast out.³² And I, when I am lifted up from the earth, will draw all people to myself."³³ He said this to show by what kind of death he was going to die." John 12:31-33

Question 3. According to John 12:31, what would happen when Jesus died on the cross?

_____

_____

_____

_____

The devil's influence and power have dominated for thousands of years. His deceptions have ruined many lives, destroyed many ministries, and divided many marriages. But from John 12:31, we see that the cross is the solution for humanity's problem with the devil. The cross is where the *"Seed of the woman"* crushed *"the head of the serpent"* (Genesis 3:15), dealing a deathblow to him. The cross, where Jesus Christ died outside the city of Jerusalem, is where He cast out the devil from the city of humanity, and where Christ defeated this evil one for all eternity.

I lived in sin for many years, was in bondage to the flesh, and in captivity to the devil. My sins were deep and dark, they characterized my life for a long time, and the power of the devil was seen quite clearly in me for all those years. But something happened. On the cross, Jesus Christ forgave all my sins, released me from captivity, and destroyed the power of the devil in my life. The effects of the cross of Jesus Christ—the casting out of the devil—have been applied in my heart and life by the Holy Spirit.

Question 4. According to John 12:32, what would happen when Jesus died on the cross?

_____

_____

It is this truth, among others, that the cross of Jesus Christ would draw all people, which caused Paul to cling to the cross with such tenacity and single-minded devotion. He knew that when he displayed the cross before the eyes and hearts of men and women, that God would draw them to Jesus.

The cross, to give it a metaphor, is shown to be a magnet. It has a drawing influence for those who will believe and be saved. It also has a repelling influence on those who reject eternal life. Both influences are at the cross:

> *"For the word of the cross is folly to those who are perishing, but*
> *to us who are being saved it is the power of God." 1 Cor. 1:18*

It is a mysterious thing how the cross of Christ is infused with the power of God. How He draws people to it by His Spirit is a mystery, as is how He reveals Christ in the Word to our hearts, and how He gives us faith to believe in Him. One of the verses of the hymn *I Know Whom I Have Believed* expresses it well:

> *I know not how the Spirit moves,*
> *Convincing us of sin,*
> *Revealing Jesus through the Word,*
> *Creating faith in Him*[2]

Though we do not know how God convinces of sin by His Spirit, how He reveals Christ in the Word, or how He creates faith in our hearts, yet we do know *where* this happens. It happens at the cross. As the guilty, condemned, and hopeless sinner drops to his or her knees at the foot of the cross and looks up believingly into the face of Jesus, something supernatural happens. The sinner is forgiven and accepted, cleansed, and relieved of the burden of sin, pardoned, and transformed. And the cross is not only where we find justification and acceptance with God, but it is also where we find the power to overcome sin (Romans 6:7-10).

2   https://library.timelesstruths.org/music/I_Know_Whom_I_Have_Believed/

This is the drawing influence that the cross exerts, the power of God that the cross provides. This magnet of a cross will be the subject of our study, and I have no doubt that it will draw my heart into deeper fellowship with God, and it is my prayer that the study will do the same for you.

Please examine the following story and answer the questions:

"So he went with them. And when they came to the Jordan, they cut down trees.[5] But as one was felling a log, his axe head fell into the water, and he cried out, "Alas, my master! It was borrowed."[6] Then the man of God said, "Where did it fall?" When he showed him the place, he cut off a stick and threw it in there and made the iron float.[7] And he said, "Take it up." So he reached out his hand and took it." 2 Kings 6:4-7

Question 5. According to 2 Kings 6:4-7, what happened to the axe head?

_____

_____

_____

_____

Question 6. What did the man of God use to find the axe head?

_____

_____

_____

_____

Question 7. What happened to the axe head when the stick was thrown into the water?

_____

_____

_____

_____

Dave writes, *"Ahh…I see the symbolism here. We are that axe head that has fallen into the sinful pattern of this world and are sunk in sin. Christ redeemed us and restored us back to God through the Cross. Just as the axe head floated up to the surface, so are we who are dead in our sin but then raised like Christ, in Christ, by Christ, and through Christ."*

The story in 2 Kings 6:4-7 teaches us that God cares for the smallest details of our lives. He was interested in helping the man find the axe head that was borrowed and that was lost in the water, and He is interested in and cares about us today, even the seemingly insignificant things in our lives. God was interested the other day when I lost my car keys, and when I stopped in my tracks and prayed to Him I soon found them.

But this is not the main lesson of this passage, and if we stopped here we would miss the point!

In 2 Kings 6:4-7, God somehow enabled the "stick" or the "wood" to have magnet-like qualities, so as to draw the axe head to the surface where it could be rescued and returned to its owner. We could say about this story, that that which was sunk and lost was found and raised. And God used a stick, a piece of wood, to do the drawing.

> *"And I, when I am lifted up from the earth, will draw all people to myself." He said this to show by what kind of death he was going to die." John 12:32-33*

As we prepare to study the subject of the cross of Jesus Christ, it is important to know that God works through this cross drawing people to Christ, saving them from their sins, cleansing them by His blood, and transforming them to live by His grace. We who were sunk and lost in sin are found and raised by the power of the cross.

A small company in the early days of gold mining in South Africa sank shaft after shaft in different locations, finding only a small amount of gold in each shaft. Ultimately, the prospectors discovered that all they needed to have done was to go deeper in the first shaft for, as they did so, they found gold in abundance. Roy Hession writes that he has found this to be true in the spiritual life also. "I testify that although I have tried all sorts of different shafts, hoping for greater results in my life, Christ has now become the end of all my searching. Revival for me has meant coming back to the place where I first began, and I intend to stay there. Tell me not of any other way. I need to go deeper at His cross—much deeper."[3]

Now we understand why Paul decided to know nothing but Jesus Christ and Him crucified, and why He proclaimed the cross at every opportunity, boasted in the cross, and worshipped at the cross.

My friend, it is my aim and purpose to "go deeper at His cross—much deeper" in this study. I hope you will come with me, and that we will enjoy the "gold in abundance" that is found at the foot of the cross.

Question 8. What are your final thoughts about today's lesson?

_____

_____

_____

_____

Mark writes, *"I was intrigued by the closeness of texts between the cross and the power of God. I had not noticed this before. Everything is centered upon the cross, everything for our salvation. But seeing it in the word like that was new. I ask myself, 'What is in the cross that draws?' Ultimately, it is the coming together at one point of all God's plans for redemption, and so at the cross,*

---

3   https://e-sword.net/, 2000+ Bible Illustrations

God's glory is best revealed. We wonder how, why, what motivated the cross, and it comes back to the glory of God. Such is His glory that He would plan the cross of Jesus Christ. What greater thing could one study! Thanks for this intro—my mind is stirred and my heart, too."

The Foundation of Our Study

Christians should be free from all habitual sin. This is stated many places in Scripture, but the book of 1 John, which was written, "that we might know that we have eternal life" (1 John 5:13), states this truth clearly:

> *This is the message we have heard from him and proclaim to you, that God is light, and in him is no darkness at all.⁶ If we say we have fellowship with him while we walk in darkness, we lie and do not practice the truth.⁷ But if we walk in the light, as he is in the light, we have fellowship with one another, and the blood of Jesus his Son cleanses us from all sin. 1 John 1:5-7*

When we talk about "habitual sin" we are referring here to sin that has become a persistent habit. We are not referring to sin that happens occasionally, but rather we are referring to sin that is practiced often. Some might use the term "life-dominating sin" here, or even sin that has "mastered" us and taken us "captive." "Habitual sin", as shown in 1 John 1:5-7 is described as "walking in darkness", and the opposite as "practicing the truth". The metaphor of "walking" indicates the direction of one's life.

Another good definition of "habitual sin" can be seen in 1 John 3:6-9:

> *"No one who abides in him keeps on sinning; no one who keeps on sinning has either seen him or known him.⁷ Little children, let no one deceive you. Whoever practices righteousness is righteous, as he is righteous.⁸ Whoever makes a practice of sinning is of the devil, for the devil has been sinning from the beginning. The reason the Son of God appeared was to destroy the works of the*

devil.⁹ No one born of God makes a practice of sinning, for God's
seed abides in him, and he cannot keep on sinning because he
has been born of God." 1 John 3:6-9

This passage defines "habitual sin" as the "practice of sinning", or that sin which has become a habit or pattern in one's life.

Question 1. According to 1 John 3:9, what is true of someone who is "born of God"?

We must distinguish between sin, which all Christians commit, and habitual sinning, in which no Christian should be involved. Again, 1 John makes this distinction clear:

"If we say we have fellowship with him while we walk in darkness,
we lie and do not practice the truth.⁷ But if we walk in the light,
as he is in the light, we have fellowship with one another, and
the blood of Jesus his Son cleanses us from all sin.⁸ If we say we
have no sin, we deceive ourselves, and the truth is not in us.⁹
If we confess our sins, he is faithful and just to forgive us our
sins and to cleanse us from all unrighteousness.¹⁰ If we say we
have not sinned, we make him a liar, and his word is not in us."
1 John 1:6-10

On the one hand, if we *"walk in the darkness"* that is, practice habitual sin, we lie and do not practice truth, on the other hand, if we *"say we have no sin"* that is if we say we have reached sinless perfection, then *"we deceive ourselves"* and the truth is not in us.

The Christian who lives in Christ cannot, at the same time, live in sin. While he can certainly stumble and fall to sin, he cannot live in habitual, life-dominating sin if he is "abiding in Him."

So, the point is this: all Christians sin (become tripped up, stumble and fall, etc.), but no Christian should live ("walk") in any habitual sin. In other words, the believer's life should not be *characterized* by sin, but by righteousness.

It is my premise in this writing that to truly overcome habitual sin, we must focus on and glory in the cross of Jesus Christ. Paul connects this cross-focus with overcoming the world in Galatians 6:14:

> *"But far be it from me to boast except in the cross of our Lord Jesus Christ, by which the world has been crucified to me, and I to the world." Galatians 6:14*

Question 2. According to Galatians 6:14, what did the cross do for Paul? What do you think this means?

_____

_____

_____

_____

Daniel writes, *"The world crucified to Paul means that everything that he once counted important and glamorous in the world is nothing more than rubbish. Paul dying to the world means that he is no longer a friend of the world and an enemy of God, but is now a friend of God and an enemy of the world. He is dead to the world and its sinful offers and way of living."*

Paul stated that through the cross, the world was crucified to him, and he to the world. In the lives of believers, there is a double crucifixion: I died to the world, and the world died to me. Through seeing the beauty and glory of the cross, the world lost all its luster and shine for Paul. The same is true for us. It is possible to become so taken up with the cross of Jesus Christ that sin, the world, the flesh, and the devil all die! We can see such beams of glory emanating from the cross that we can scarcely take it in, and we end up losing ourselves in the love of God. This was the experience of the hymn-writer of *How Great Thou Art*:

And when I think of God, His Son not sparing;
Sent Him to die, I scarce can take it in,
That on the cross, my burden gladly bearing;
He bled and died to take away my sin.[4]

The gospel of God's grace, which is centered in the cross of Jesus Christ, contains liberating power for all who come to believe. This power is sufficient to save any sinner, justify all the ungodly, sanctify all justified sinners, and glorify every sanctified saint.

"For the word of the cross is folly to those who are perishing, but to us who are being saved it is the power of God." 1 Corinthians 1:18

Question 3. What two types of people are listed in 1 Corinthians 1:18? What are the different reactions evidenced by each of them?

_____

_____

_____

_____

Matt writes, *"Those who reject the cross find it offensive and foolishness. Those who humbly accept the Gospel message see their own sinfulness and depravity and know that it is the only way to be saved; that works will get them nowhere."*

The Greek word translated as "power" in 1 Corinthians 1:18 is *"dunamis"* from where we get our word "dynamite." The cross of Jesus Christ contains explosive

4   https://hymnary.org/text/o_lord_my_god_when_i_in_awesome_wonder

power to save us from our sins, to knock down every evil stronghold, to give repentance to hardened sinners, to defeat the power of the evil one in our lives.

So, in truth, as we set out on this study of the cross we can expect to come to know, and experience, the power of God in a much more profound way. This should create anticipation in our hearts, knowing that we are embarking on a journey that connects us with the power of God through the cross of Christ.

Paul said the gospel was of *"utmost importance"*:

> *"Now I would remind you, brothers, of the gospel I preached to you, which you received, in which you stand,² and by which you are being saved if you hold fast to the word I preached to you—unless you believed in vain.³ For I delivered to you as of first importance what I also received: that Christ died for our sins in accordance with the Scriptures,⁴ that he was buried, that he was raised on the third day in accordance with the Scriptures," 1 Corinthians 15:1-4*

Question 4. According to 1 Corinthians 15:3-4, what is of first importance?

_____

_____

_____

_____

Question 5. According to 1 Corinthians 15:3-4, what is the gospel?

_____

_____

_____

_____

In 1 Corinthians 15:1-4, Paul declares that the death, burial, and resurrection of Jesus Christ is of first importance. Therefore it should thoroughly excite us that we are studying the most important event and teaching in Scripture, and we should expect to experience the power of God as we focus on the cross of Christ.

Our intention in this study is to be like the four women in John 19:25: *"but standing by the cross of Jesus were his mother and his mother's sister, Mary the wife of Clopas, and Mary Magdalene." John 19:25*

These four women were *"standing by the cross"* taking it all in, heartbroken at the sight of it, yet pondering in their hearts the meaning of it. When all the other disciples had deserted Jesus, these four remained, and as they *"stood by the cross,"* they heard words of blessing and instruction from Jesus' mouth: *"Father, forgive them..." "Woman, behold your son," "It is finished,"* etc.

Our hope and earnest expectation are likewise to stand by the cross and hear words of blessing and instruction that only those who linger by the cross will hear. The words of blessing that we will hear will be a balm to the sinner's heart, encouragement to the weary, strength for the weak, medicine for the spiritually ill, and vitality to the souls of all who will listen. Words such as these will ring in our hearts, *"today you will be with me in Paradise"*, *"He reconciled us to God... through the cross"* (Eph. 2:16), *"He made peace by the blood of His cross"* (Col. 1:20), *"He canceled the record of debt...nailing it to the cross"* (Col. 2:14), and many more.

Our method in this study will be to ponder the event of the cross itself, to consider the clear statements made in the New Testament about the cross, to view the portraits of the cross that are scattered throughout the Old Testament and to examine the prophetic writings about the death of Jesus. Through it all, we will always seek to apply the cross to our own lives.

Christians should not live in habitual sin; Scripture makes this clear. But the only true and biblical method of overcoming habitual sin in our lives is through the power of the cross of Jesus Christ. Do we want to repent of gluttony? Then we must study the cross. Do we want to be free from laziness? Then we must view the cross and contemplate it. Do we want to be free from pornography and all impurity, from drunkenness and drugs, from bitterness, greed, sinful anger and rage, gossip, slander, and covetousness? Then we must focus on the cross of Jesus Christ and experience its power.

Oh, what incredible power, grace, and love are displayed to believers in the cross of Jesus Christ. When was the last time you pondered the cross to such an extent that it dissolved your heart in thankfulness and brought your eyes to tears? This is a real experience that can be had by all who will "stand by the cross" of Christ and linger. One hymn writer stated how the cross changed his affections in this way:

Was it for crimes that I had done, He groaned upon the tree?
Amazing pity! grace unknown! And love beyond degree!

Well, might the sun in darkness hide And shut his glories in,
When Christ, the mighty Maker died, For man the creature's sin.

Thus might I hide my blushing face While His dear cross appears,
Dissolve my heart in thankfulness, And melt my eyes to tears.[5]

This can be our experience, too, as we enter into the suffering, death, and resurrection of Jesus Christ and examine the results of the cross in our lives.

As this lesson ends, will you stop and pray this prayer with me, in anticipation of what we will experience through this study?

Draw me nearer, nearer blessed Lord,
To the cross where Thou hast died.
Draw me nearer, nearer, nearer blessed Lord,
To Thy precious, bleeding side[6]

Question 6. What are your goals as you study through this book?

_____

_____

_____

_____

5   https://hymnary.org/text/alas_and_did_my_savior_bleed

6   https://hymnary.org/text/i_am_thine_o_lord_i_have_heard_thy_voice

LESSON 3:

The Historical and Prophetic
Evidence of the Cross

*T*he cross and resurrection of Jesus was an actual, historically verifiable event. There really was a man named Jesus Christ Who lived His life in the Middle East doing good to all people, who was, near the end of His life, beaten and bruised, flogged and scourged, and then hung up on a Roman cross between two criminals, and then rose from the dead three days later. Christians do not have blind faith, but rather belief centered in biblical truth and historical evidence. The record is given to us in all four gospels:

> *"And when they came to a place called Golgotha (which means Place of a Skull),[34] they offered him wine to drink, mixed with gall, but when he tasted it, he would not drink it.[35] And when they had crucified him, they divided his garments among them by casting lots.[36] Then they sat down and kept watch over him there.[37] And over his head they put the charge against him, which read, "This is Jesus, the King of the Jews."[38] Then two robbers were crucified with him, one on the right and one on the left." Matthew 27:33-38*

> *"And they crucified him and divided his garments among them, casting lots for them, to decide what each should take.[25] And it was the third hour when they crucified him.[26] And the inscription of the charge against him read, "The King of the Jews."[27] And with him they crucified two robbers, one on his right and one on his left." Mark 15:24-27*

"Two others, who were criminals, were led away to be put to death with him.³³ And when they came to the place that is called The Skull, there they crucified him, and the criminals, one on his right and one on his left." Luke 23:32-33

"...and he went out, bearing his own cross, to the place called the place of a skull, which in Aramaic is called Golgotha. There they crucified him, and with him two others, one on either side, and Jesus between them." John 19:17-18

Josh McDowell is a Christian evidence writer and lecturer. He works with Campus Crusade for Christ International and often speaks to college and university students. In his book, *Evidence that Demands a Verdict*, he has a chapter entitled, "Jesus a Man of History." Part of that chapter is a section called "Non-Biblical sources for the historicity of Jesus." In it, he quotes Tacitus, Josephus, Pliny's letter to Trajan, and others. He cites about seven sources from the first century, which refer to the life, death, and resurrection of Jesus Christ. And Josh is just one of many writers who have compiled extensive documentation related to Christ's life, death, and resurrection.[7]

No, our faith is not "blind," but instead, based on the evidence which God reveals to us in His Word, which can be verified through research.

The crucifixion of Jesus Christ is not only historically verifiable, but it is also prophetically reliable. The Old Testament foretold the death of Jesus Christ in great detail. Before we look at some of these texts, we need to see a key passage in the New Testament that helps us understand the Old Testament:

"Concerning this salvation, the prophets who prophesied about the grace that was to be yours searched and inquired carefully,¹¹ inquiring what person or time the Spirit of Christ in them was indicating when he predicted the sufferings of Christ and the subsequent glories.¹² It was revealed to them that they were serving not themselves but you, in the things that have now been announced to you through those who preached the good news to you by the Holy Spirit sent from heaven, things into which angels long to look." 1 Peter 1:10-12

7   Josh McDowell, *Evidence that Demands a Verdict,* Campus Crusade for Christ International, 1972

Question 1. According to 1 Peter 1:11, what did the Spirit of Christ in the Old Testament prophets predict?

_____

_____

_____

_____

1 Peter 1:10-12 is a key passage because it tells us that the Spirit of Christ was in the Old Testament prophets, predicting the suffering, death, resurrection, and subsequent glories of Jesus Christ. And when the prophets inquired as to the timing of the suffering Messiah, they were informed that it was to be in the future, that is, in the time when Jesus would be born, die on the cross, rise from the dead, and ascend into heaven.

Let's keep this in mind as we now review some of the passages that the Old Testament prophets wrote, in which we can see the suffering, death, and resurrection of the Messiah Who was to come:

> "I am poured out like water, and all my bones are out of joint; my heart is like wax; it is melted within my breast;[15] my strength is dried up like a potsherd, and my tongue sticks to my jaws; you lay me in the dust of death.[16] For dogs encompass me; a company of evildoers encircles me; they have pierced my hands and feet-[17] I can count all my bones- they stare and gloat over me;[18] they divide my garments among them, and for my clothing they cast lots." Psalm 22:14-18

Question 2. Please consider Psalm 22:14-18, and then list the ways in which this passage describes the crucifixion of Jesus Christ.

_____

_____

_____

_____

"By oppression and judgment he was taken away and as for his generation, who considered that he was cut off out of the land of the living, stricken for the transgression of my people?⁹ And they made his grave with the wicked and with a rich man in his death, although he had done no violence, and there was no deceit in his mouth." Isaiah 53:8-9

Question 3. Please consider Isaiah 53:8-9, and then list the ways in which this passage describes the crucifixion of Jesus Christ.

_____

_____

_____

_____

Question 4. Isaiah 53:8 tells us why Jesus Christ was "stricken"; in other words, why Jesus died on the cross. In verse 8, what specific words tell us plainly why Jesus died?

_____

_____

_____

_____

There are many more passages of Scripture which prophetically describe the crucifixion of the Messiah, detailing in advance His suffering, His death, and His resurrection. Moses said one like himself was coming, a prophet to whom the people must listen (Deuteronomy 18:15), and Stephen points out in Acts 7 that God's people rejected Moses when he tried to help them. Then, at his second coming (after his forty years in the desert), God's people embraced Moses as their leader (Acts 7:25-36). Jesus Himself said that the Scriptures "testify of me" (John 5:39), and on the Emmaus road, He took His troubled and discouraged disciples to God's Word and explained everything in the Scriptures "concerning Himself" (Luke 24:27). The following passages have a direct reference to the cross of Jesus Christ: Genesis 3:15, Exodus 12:1-51, Numbers 21:5-9, Ruth 3-4, Esther 7:10, Job 19:25, Psalm 22, and numerous others. Indeed, the whole of the Old Testament makes up one body of evidence for the substitutionary death of Jesus for our sins and His bodily resurrection from the dead.

So, before we begin considering the biblical record and studying further the "why" of Jesus' death, it is essential to understand that the Old Testament foretold the cross, which was fulfilled and recorded in the New Testament and is historically verifiable by both religious and non-religious writings. The faith of Christians in the death of Christ rests on the revealed truth of God's Word and can be verified historically in numerous ways.

> *"Now faith is the substance of things hoped for, the evidence of things not seen" (Hebrews 11:1 NKJV)*

Hebrews 11:1 tells us that real saving faith has *"substance"* and *"evidence"* with which to believe. The disciple Thomas doubted, and Jesus provided evidence by presenting the wounds in His pierced hands and side. In the same way, God's Word gives us ample data and proof of Jesus' death on our behalf, and His resurrection from the dead, which can be substantiated and confirmed in numerous ways. This is important because God makes believing in Jesus, and specifically in His death and resurrection, the condition for our salvation:

> *Whoever believes in the Son has eternal life; whoever does not obey the Son shall not see life, but the wrath of God remains on him. John 3:36*

In John 3, we read of an encounter between Jesus and a very prominent religious teacher of that day named Nicodemus. Jesus told Nicodemus that for a man to be saved, he must be born again (John 3:3), which left Nicodemus wondering how that could be. Jesus then referenced the Old Testament Scriptures with which Nicodemus was very familiar, and made an analogy that pointed directly to Jesus' upcoming death on the cross:

> *"And as Moses lifted up the serpent in the wilderness, so must the Son of Man be lifted up, that whoever believes in him may have eternal life." John 3:14-15*

Jesus took Nicodemus to a story from the historical past of the nation of Israel. The situation was that the Israelites were complaining against Moses, so God sent serpents among them. The snakes were biting and killing the Israelites, so Moses cried out to God for deliverance. In response to that call for help, God told Moses to erect a pole and place a snake on it, and all who looked at the snake would live. Jesus summarized and applied that historical event to His cross. He said that He, like that serpent, must be lifted, that whoever believes in Him would not perish, but would have eternal life (John 3:16).

We will examine this story in detail in another lesson, but, for now, we should understand that the Old Testament points forward to and speaks directly about the cross of Jesus Christ. It does this in story form (like the story of the serpents in Numbers 21) and by direct and clear prophetic statements (like Isaiah 53).

Let's consider John 3:36 again:

> *"Whoever believes in the Son has eternal life; whoever does not obey the Son shall not see life, but the wrath of God remains on him." John 3:36*

John 3:36 tells us that believing in Jesus is that which both removes the wrath of God from us and grants us eternal life. God makes believing in His Son that important. And if believing in Christ is that important, then God in His grace provides us with *"substance"* and *"evidence"* to believe; in other words, through His Word, He shows us the *"scars in His hands, the hole in His side, the marks on His feet,"* and instructs us *"do not be unbelieving, but believing"* (John 20:27).

Question 5. According to John 3:36, what transpires when a person comes to faith in Jesus Christ?

_____

_____

_____

_____

Question 6. According to John 3:36, what remains on the person who refuses to obey God by believing in His Son?

_____

_____

_____

_____

Question 7. Are you a believer in Jesus Christ? Specifically, have you looked to His death on the cross to provide the cure for your sin, just as the Israelites were to look to the snake on the pole for their cure? If you are a believer in Jesus Christ, are you now looking to the cross for continued freedom from the power of sin in your life?

_____

_____

_____

Kathy writes, _"I am a believer in Jesus Christ. He died on the cross to pay the penalty for my sins against a Holy God and I humbled myself before Him and asked Him to save me and_ *forgive me. I have not been taught about looking to the Cross for continued freedom from the power of sin in my life. I now know what has been missing, and I am so hungry to learn what this study is going to teach me."*

This is an important issue. Sin has *One Remedy*, which can be found only in the death of Jesus Christ. Our self-effort, will power, resolutions, and promises to do better mean nothing in the fight for freedom from habitual sin. Only the cross with all its power to forgive and cleanse, remove guilt and shame, and provide new life can supply us with the real and lasting solution to habitual sin.

The hymn *Rock of Ages* presents this "cure" very clearly:

> *Rock of Ages, cleft for me,*
> *Let me hide myself in Thee;*
> *Let the water and the blood,*
> *From Thy wounded side which flowed,*
> *Be of sin the double cure; Save from*
> *wrath and make me pure.*
>
> *Nothing in my hand I bring,*
> *Simply to the cross I cling;*
> *Naked, come to Thee for dress;*
> *Helpless look to Thee for grace;*
> *Foul, I to the fountain fly;*
> *Wash me, Savior, or I die*[8]

My friend, there is abundant and ample evidence for believing in Jesus Christ. The cross of Christ is central to all of Scripture and has been called "the scarlet cord" that runs through every page of the Bible. It is our hope in this study to trace that beautiful scarlet cord as it weaves through the stories and wraps around the prophetic writings of the Old Testament, and as it is displayed brilliantly with clear statements in the New Testament.

---

8   https://hymnary.org/text/rock_of_ages_cleft_for_me_let_me_hide

Question 8. What thoughts do you have as you contemplate working through the rest of these lessons on the cross of Jesus Christ?

_____

_____

_____

_____

I hope that you are filled with anticipation, as I am, to come to the cross and to see God's glory in the death of His Son. I pray that together we would grow in our love for Jesus Christ as we examine His cross and that we would resolve like Paul both to know nothing but Jesus Christ and Him crucified and to boast only in that cross.

The Glorious Display of God's Righteousness

*D*id you know that at the cross, we see the fullest expression of the character of God? At the cross, we see His justice, His wrath and hatred, His love and pity, His righteousness, forgiveness, mercy, supremacy, authority, truth, kindness, sovereignty, power, grace, longsuffering, passion, sympathy, knowledge, judgment, and many more aspects of His character.

Please study this passage of Scripture with me, and answer the questions that follow:

> *"So I am eager to preach the gospel to you also who are in Rome.[16] For I am not ashamed of the gospel, for it is the power of God for salvation to everyone who believes, to the Jew first and also to the Greek.[17] For in it the righteousness of God is revealed from faith for faith, as it is written, "The righteous shall live by faith."[18] For the wrath of God is revealed from heaven against all ungodliness and unrighteousness of men, who by their unrighteousness suppress the truth." Romans 1:15-18*

Question 1. What is the gospel, as stated by Paul in Romans 1:16?

_____

_____

_____

_____

Question 2. Please list the two things that this passage of Scripture states that the gospel "reveals" (specifically in verses 17 and 18).

_____

_____

_____

_____

In this short passage, we have seen that the gospel is the *power* of God and reveals the *righteousness* of God and the *wrath* of God.

It is clear that on the cross, Jesus Christ displayed the glory of the character of God. According to Romans 1:15-18, the cross/resurrection event evidences the power, righteousness, and wrath of God, among other things. These are the truths we will study in this lesson.

Question 3. Right now, please think through and write down how it is that the gospel is the power of God and how it displays the wrath of God and the righteousness of God.

_____

_____

_____

_____

Jeff writes, "*The gospel is the power of God in that it is the true story of how God came to earth in the Person of His Son the Lord Jesus Christ, and after living a perfectly sinless life, Jesus obeyed His Father and gave His life for us at Calvary in order that all our sin could be judged and punished eternally as He was our Sin-Bearer/ Sacrificial Lamb who died for us!! It displays the wrath of God in this I believe in that Jesus' death on the Cross truly shows how serious sin is and how a Holy and loving God displayed all of this!*"

The **power** of God is seen at the cross, as God draws sinners to Himself through the forgiveness of their sin, removal of their guilt, and complete changing of their nature. The **righteousness** of God is seen at the cross, as God punishes sin by giving His only Son to die. God does not overlook sin, for if He did, He would not be righteous. No, God punishes sin. God is righteous. And the **wrath** of God is shown at the cross as God pummels His Son with wave after wave of His wrath, and He turns His face away from Christ, the Sin-bearer.

The following passages of Scripture, though experienced by the authors, find their fullest and final expression in Jesus Christ. The Spirit of Jesus in these prophets was "pointing forward to the sufferings of Christ..." (1 Peter 1:11).

"Deep calls to deep at the roar of your waterfalls; all your breakers and your wave have gone over me." Psalm 42:7

"Your wrath lies heavy upon me, and you overwhelm me with all your waves. Selah" Psalm 88:7

"For the arrows of the Almighty are in me; my spirit drinks their poison; the terrors of God are arrayed against me." Job 6:4

"He has prepared for him his deadly weapons, making his arrows fiery shafts." Psalm 7:13

"For your arrows have sunk into me, and your hand has come down on me." Psalm 38:2

Next, let us examine Romans 3:21-26:

"But now the righteousness of God has been manifested apart from the law, although the Law and the Prophets bear witness to it-[22] the righteousness of God through faith in Jesus Christ for all who believe. For there is no distinction:[23] for all have sinned and fall short of the glory of God,[24] and are justified by his grace as a gift, through the redemption that is in Christ Jesus,[25] whom

God put forward as a propitiation by his blood, to be received by faith. This was to show God's righteousness, because in his divine forbearance he had passed over former sins.[26] It was to show his righteousness at the present time, so that he might be just and the justifier of the one who has faith in Jesus." Romans 3:21-26

Question 4. Romans 3:25 tells us what characteristic of God that the cross reveals clearly. What is it? The cross was "to show God's..."

_____

_____

_____

_____

Question 5. Romans 3:26 says "it was to show His righteousness..." To what does the "it" refer to in Romans 3:25?

_____

_____

_____

In Romans 3:21-26, Paul is comparing the law and the cross, the Old Covenant and the New Covenant. He states that the righteousness of God is revealed *"apart from the law,"* but that the law and the prophets testify of this righteousness. The righteousness of God is revealed *"through the redemption that is in Christ Jesus"* not through the law. Jesus was put forward as *"a propitiation"* (removal of God's wrath) by His blood.

The statement that Jesus "propitiated" God's wrath speaks volumes. It says that at the cross, Jesus was the recipient of all of God's hatred toward sin.

On behalf of believers, Jesus took the full force and brunt of God's wrath, that God's wrath might be turned away from all who believe.

There is a most instructive illustration of this "propitiation" in the Old Testament. Remember that "the law and the prophets bear witness" to this "propitiation" and righteousness of God in the cross. The illustration that teaches this truth so beautifully is in the Book of Esther.

We remember from studying the Book of Esther that Haman plotted the death of all the Jews, but that his evil plot was discovered. Mordecai told Esther about the plot and encouraged her to intercede on behalf of God's people, as they were now under a death sentence. Esther sought help from the king, and when King Ahasuerus was informed of the plot to kill the Jews, his anger was stirred up against Haman. The Bible records it this way:

> "And the king arose in his wrath from the wine-drinking and went into the palace garden, but Haman stayed to beg for his life from Queen Esther, for he saw that harm was determined against him by the king" (Esther 7:7).

The king stormed out mad, full of wrath, determined to bring harm to Haman. And when he returned, a servant conveniently suggested that there had been a gallows already built, upon which Haman had planned to hang Mordecai. Then this amazing statement is made:

> And the king said, "Hang him (Haman) on that." So they hanged Haman on the gallows that he had prepared for Mordecai. Then the wrath of the king abated. Esther 7:10

> **Question 6.** The word in Esther 7:10 "abated" means that the wrath of the king subsided, or that he was appeased, that his wrath was assuaged. What event in this story abated the wrath of the king, as stated by the word "then" in Esther 7:10?

_____

_____

_____

_____

Ah, and here we have it: the picture of the cross and its effects. When Haman died on the wooden gallows, the wrath of the king subsided. And while this "foreshadow" is incomplete (as all shadows are), it does show that the hanging of the man on the wood satisfied the wrath of the king, which points forward to how God would be "propitiated by His blood" as recorded in Romans 3:25. In the story of Esther, the wrath of the king against Haman subsided when Haman died on the gallows; in the gospel, the wrath of the king against all believers was fully propitiated when Jesus Christ died on the cross. If you are a believer, look at the cross and see that God will never be angry with you for His anger and wrath was fully exhausted at the cross. Jesus *"saves us from the wrath* (for unbelievers) *to come"* (1 Thessalonians 1:10).

> *"In this is love, not that we have loved God but that he loved us*
> *and sent his Son to be the propitiation for our sins." 1 John 4:10*

"Must a guilty man remain under the wrath of Almighty God? Is the wound of sin forever incurable? No, there is a Savior provided for us in Christ. Matthew Henry says, "This is the righteousness of God; righteousness of his ordaining, providing, and accepting."[9]

> *"Christ redeemed us from the curse of the law by becoming a curse*
> *for us—for it is written, "Cursed is everyone who is hanged on a*
> *tree..." Galatians 3:13*

It is in the seeing of this Savior receiving the wrath of God that produces hymns like *Alas! and Did My Savior Bleed* with verses like this:

> *"Thy body slain, sweet Jesus, Thine,*
> *And bathed in its own blood;*
> *While all exposed to wrath divine,*
> *The glorious Sufferer stood."[10]*

---

9   https://biblehub.com/commentaries/mhc/romans/3.htm

10   https://hymnary.org/text/alas_and_did_my_savior_bleed

I don't know about you, but right about now, I don't know whether to cry my eyes out or shout, "Hallelujah!" The fact that the wrath of God against us for all our grievous sins has been fully exhausted in Jesus Christ on the cross should make us want to weep with joy and relief, and the truth that there is no wrath left for us should make us want to shout "Hallelujah"! Jesus took all the arrows of God's hatred in our place. It should break our hearts and then fill them with songs of rejoicing to know that God poured out wave after wave of His wrath upon His Son until finally, the flood subsided entirely. There are no more arrows or waves left for us. While we were *"at one time, objects of wrath"* (Ephesians 2:3) we are now *"vessels of mercy"* (Romans 9:23) for the wrath of God is fully spent on Christ, and God *"made us alive"* (Ephesians 2:5) and *"raised us up"* (Ephesians 2:6). *"There is therefore now no condemnation for those who are in Christ Jesus"* (Romans 8:1). Praise God!

And God, in all this, declares His righteousness. We can understand that God hates sin when nothing less than the blood of Jesus Christ could pay for it.

So, we have seen that the cross displays and reveals the wrath of God, and the righteousness of God. Now let us examine how it shows the power of God:

> **"***For Christ did not send me to baptize but to preach the gospel, and not with words of eloquent wisdom, lest the cross of Christ be emptied of its power.[18] For the word of the cross is folly to those who are perishing, but to us who are being saved it is the power of God."* 1 Corinthians 1:17-18

Question 7. According to 1 Corinthians 1:17-18, what would have happened had Paul preached baptism as a way of salvation rather than the cross?

_____

_____

_____

_____

Question 8. What is the cross to us who are being saved?

_____

_____

_____

_____

This passage in 1 Corinthians has reference to both unbelievers and believers. Paul states clearly that the cross of Jesus Christ has the power to save sinners, which is why he preaches the cross and not baptism nor any works of any kind that we do. We become saved when, at the cross of Jesus Christ, we find forgiveness for our sins, healing for our broken hearts, and new life in Jesus Christ. But the passage also refers to believers, clearly stating that the cross is the power of God *"to us who are being saved."*

In other words, the cross has the power of God to convert sinners, but also the cross is the power of God for believers. The cross not only saves us from the penalty of sin, but it also breaks the power of sin as well. Unlike those who teach that the cross is merely to get unbelievers converted, and then we move on "to the deeper teachings," Paul's point is that the cross is powerful for both unbelievers and believers. We remember Paul saying, as a believer, that the world was crucified to him, and he to the world through the cross (Galatians 6:14). The cross is the power of God both for the salvation of unbelievers and the sanctification of believers.

So, we have seen today that the cross reveals the wrath of God, the righteousness of God, and the power of God. The cross displays the fierce hatred of God against sin vividly. It shows the righteousness of God, for God did not leave sin unpunished but required Jesus' blood in payment. It shows the power of God, for God uses the cross to grant forgiveness to those who repent, to bring them from death to life, to break the power of sin in their lives, and to send them on their way rejoicing in the Lord.

A Bible-believing Christian once was assailed by an atheist who said, "I don't understand how the blood of Jesus Christ can wash away my sin, nor do I believe it."

"You and Paul agree on that," answered the Bible student.

"How so?" replied the atheist.

"1 Corinthians 1:18 says, 'For the preaching of the cross is to them that perish foolishness, but unto us which are saved it is the power of God.' "

The atheist looked startled and then contemplatively began to study the Bible, where he soon found the cross to be the power of God unto his salvation. What POWER there is in the cross of Jesus Christ.

Question 9. As you contemplate the wrath and righteousness of God and the power of the cross, what final thoughts come to mind? Please share:

_____

_____

_____

_____

Andrew writes, "*I never viewed the cross before as Jesus being the target of God's wrath to fulfill the righteous requirements of the law. The passages in Psalms are clear illustrations of this. I also never really thought about the cross being necessary to fulfill God's own righteousness. God set up his holy requirements, and only he could fulfill them and meet them in an awesome display of his love for us. This is going much deeper than I could have imagined. Finally, the cross being the power of God for believers is awesome. I, too, have moved away from the cross after "knowledge" of salvation. I say knowledge because I still lived in sin until I took the purity courses at Setting Captives Free. It is the very cross that saves me and gives me the power to continue to resist sin for God's glory. I'm starting to get it slowly. God is so good, so wise. Thank you, Jesus, for bearing the wrath of God's arrows for me.*"

The Glorious Display of God's Mercy, Love, and Grace

*I*n lesson 4, our study took us to passages of Scripture that reveal God's power, His wrath against sin, and His righteousness as exhibited in the cross of Jesus Christ. Today, we want to examine the love of God. In the next lesson, we will study His grace, mercy, and kindness, which are most clearly portrayed in the death of Jesus.

> *"For God so loved the world, that he gave his only Son, that whoever believes in him should not perish but have eternal life." John 3:16*

> *"Greater love has no one than this, that someone lays down his life for his friends." John 15:13*

> *"...but God shows his love for us in that while we were still sinners, Christ died for us." Romans 5:8*

> *"It is no longer I who live, but Christ who lives in me. And the life I now live in the flesh I live by faith in the Son of God, who loved me and gave himself for me." Galatians 2:20*

> *"And walk in love, as Christ loved us and gave himself up for us, a fragrant offering and sacrifice to God." Ephesians 5:2*

> *"Husbands, love your wives, as Christ loved the church and gave himself up for her," Ephesians 5:25*

*"In this is love, not that we have loved God but that he loved us
and sent his Son to be the propitiation for our sins." 1 John 4:10*

The cross displays the love of God, the Father, and the love of Jesus Christ for us in blazing glory. Never has passionate love reached such a fervor, never has love been displayed with such dedication and zeal and commitment. God *loves* us, so Jesus died for us. Jesus *loves* us, so He gave up His life willingly for us. It is a simple truth, but this truth has been saving and changing lives for thousands of years.

But to understand and embrace the love of God thoroughly, we must understand the *need* for the cross better. We learned in lesson 4 that God hates sin, and that because of His righteousness, He must punish sin. We read of God's further detestation of sin in Habakkuk 1:13:

"You who are of purer eyes than to see evil and cannot look at wrong, why do you idly look at traitors and are silent when the wicked swallows up the man more righteous than he?" Habakkuk 1:13

God cannot even look at wrong. He is too pure to see evil. He hates sin so much that He cannot look at it. And since all people are born sinners (Psalm 51:5; Romans 3:10; Romans 3:23), God's righteousness and purity will not allow Him to look upon us, much less allow us into His presence.

Psalm 7:11 states that "*...God is angry with the wicked every day*" (KJV).

Romans 1:18 is particularly clear on this subject:

"For the wrath of God is revealed from heaven against all ungodliness and unrighteousness of men, who by their unrighteousness suppress the truth." Romans 1:18

Question 1. What does Romans 1:18 say is revealed from heaven against all ungodliness and unrighteousness of men?

But God also loves the world (John 3:16). So, how can God's hatred for sin and wickedness, His anger for the wicked, His wrath against the unrighteousness of men, and His love for the world be harmonized and reconciled? It is an important question.

The answer is that through the cross of Christ, God's wrath is appeased, His anger at the unrighteous deeds of sinful man is expressed and exhausted, but His love is also displayed in all of its beauty and for all eternity. At the cross, the love of God for sinners finds full expression. At the cross, God can be just and the justifier of the ungodly (Romans 3:26). Because of the death of Jesus Christ, God's love triumphs and extends throughout all eternity for those who believe in Jesus Christ.

This kind of love caused Paul to erupt in praise as He tries to put dimensions around the love of Christ:

> "so that Christ may dwell in your hearts through faith-that you, being rooted and grounded in love,[18] may have strength to comprehend with all the saints what is the breadth and length and height and depth,[19] and to know the love of Christ that surpasses knowledge, that you may be filled with all the fullness of God." Ephesians 3:17-19

Question 2. What does Ephesians 3:17-19 teach about the love of God?

_____

_____

_____

_____

According to Ephesians 3:17-19, the love of God found at the cross of Christ is both an experiential love and a filling love. We can "know" by experiencing the love of Christ through His suffering and death, and the experiential knowledge of His love will flood our souls with all of God's fullness.

Have you meditated on the amazing love of God as shown in the death of His Son? Have you thought about how much love God has that He would send His only Son to die in your place? Have you meditated about the love of Christ Who suffered willingly and died substitutionally, because He loves us eternally? Oh, what wonder is found in contemplating the eternal love of God in Jesus Christ as exhibited at His death!

Country music artist George Strait sings a song entitled, "Love without End, Amen." It tells the story of a young boy coming home from school after having a fight and expecting punishment from his dad. Fully expecting the wrath of his father, the son waited, expecting the worst. However, the father said, "Let me tell you a secret about a father's love ...Daddies don't just love their children every now and then ...it's a love without end. Amen."

The young lad grew up and passed this secret on to his children. One day he dreamed that he died and went to heaven. He was concerned, as he waited to go in, because he realized there must be some mistake for if they knew half the things he's done they would never let him in. It was then that he heard his father's words again, "Let me tell you a secret about a father's love ...Daddies don't just love their children every now and then ...it's a love without end. Amen."[11]

George's song isn't precise theologically, but it is comforting to know that those who have repented of their sin and have trusted Christ for salvation have a Father whose love is unending! It is no secret, concerning our Father's love: God doesn't just love His children every now and then; indeed, it is a "love without end, Amen." Just look at the cross, and you'll see God's full commitment to love you to the end and beyond!

> "Before the Passover celebration, Jesus knew that his hour had come to leave this world and return to his Father. He had loved his disciples during his ministry on earth, and now **he loved them to the very end.**" John 13:1 (NLT)

---

11   Bill Thrasher, 2,000+ Bible Illustrations, www.e-sword.net

Please read the following Scriptures and answer the questions below:

"In this the love of God was made manifest among us, that God sent his only Son into the world, so that we might live through him." 1 John 4:9

Question 3. According to 1 John 4:9, how is the love of God "made manifest" (revealed) among us?

_____

_____

_____

_____

This passage in 1 John 4:9 tells us that the cross displays, or *"makes manifest"* the love of God. Indeed, it does, for one must love supremely to give up his life for another.

"He who did not spare his own Son but gave him up for us all, how will he not also with him graciously give us all things?[33] Who shall bring any charge against God's elect? It is God who justifies.[34] Who is to condemn? Christ Jesus is the one who died-more than that, who was raised-who is at the right hand of God, who indeed is interceding for us.[35] Who shall separate us from the love of Christ? Shall tribulation, or distress, or persecution, or famine, or nakedness, or danger, or sword?[36] As it is written, For your sake we are being killed all the day long; we are regarded as sheep to be slaughtered.

"No, in all these things we are more than conquerors through him who loved us.[38] For I am sure that neither death nor life, nor angels nor rulers, nor things present nor things to come, nor powers,[39] nor height nor depth, nor anything else in all creation, will be able to separate us from the love of God in Christ Jesus our Lord." Romans 8:32-39

Question 4. To what event does Romans 8:32 specifically refer?

_____

_____

_____

_____

Question 5. What does Romans 8:32 have to do with Romans 8:33-36?

_____

_____

_____

_____

Dierdre writes, *"It provides a foundation for the subsequent verses. It talks about the greatest gift and blessing we can receive is the cross. No one can bring a charge against God's people because our sins have been propitiated by His blood. He is now interceding for us at God's right hand. We cannot be separated by Christ's love no matter what."*

We notice from Romans 8:32 that the cross of Jesus Christ (God not sparing His Son) is the foundation or basis upon which God does all other things.

"...*all* the blessings we enjoy as Christian people come to us because of what happened on the cross. The cross is the most crucial event in history. It is from the cross that every benefit ultimately comes." Dr. Martyn Lloyd Jones[12]

The following five things are plainly seen from Romans 8:32-36:

1. **God *"gives us all things"* needful for our lives, based upon the foundation of the cross** where He did not spare His own Son.

---

12 *God the Father, God the Son*, Lloyd-Jones, Martin, page 353, published by Crossway Books, 2003

In other words, He didn't spare His Son (the best), so He will likewise not withhold any good thing (the rest). The cross is the foundation of His promise to provide all we need.—verse 32

2. **Christians are above accusation, based upon the work Jesus did on the cross.** Jesus Christ was accused of our sin and charged with our guilt, and put to death in our place. Nobody can charge us with any sin because our sins were charged to God's Son, and then He died for us, so no accusation against us will stand.—verse 33

3. **Christians will never be condemned.** Jesus stood in our place condemned, that we might be free not only from accusation but also from condemnation.

> *Bearing shame and scoffing rude,*
> *In my place condemned He stood;*
> *Sealed my pardon with His blood.*
> *Hallelujah! What a Savior!*[13]

The cross is the foundation for the believer's pardon. There is therefore now no condemnation for those who are in Christ Jesus (Romans 8:1).—verse 34

4. **Christians will never be separated from the love of God.** Because Jesus was separated from His Father on the cross, where He suffered and died in our place, we will never be separated from the love of Christ. Jesus will not remove His love from us if we act poorly, just as God did not give us His love because we lived rightly, but rather simply because He chose to do so for the glory of His own Name (Deuteronomy 7:7-8). So tribulation, distress, persecution, famine, nakedness, danger, and sword will not separate us from the love of Christ, and the

---

13   https://hymnary.org/text/man_of_sorrows_what_a_name

cross is the basis for this promise of God to never remove His love. This is love without end, amen!

5. **Christians are conquerors in all things—even in death**. Because Jesus died and rose again, thereby defeating sin, death, hell and the grave, Christians are now made "more than conquerors" through Him Who loved us unto death. The cross is the foundation for our triumphing in all things.—verse 37

Question 6. By way of review, please think about and write down the five blessings listed in this lesson which flow from the cross of Jesus Christ.

_____

_____

_____

_____

John writes, *"What blessings these are indeed! These five blessings are the hope that lies in each Christian and the longing that lies in each soul. We all love to be loved unconditionally, to be forgiven completely, to be accepted totally, to stand without condemnation or accusation. All of this and so much more is found in God's love for us—and to top it all off, God will never stop loving us and through this love we can find true freedom and victory."*

Oh, what love is demonstrated at the cross, and oh what blessings flow from it. The cross is the "amen" to, and the guarantee of, God's promise in Deuteronomy 7:13: *"He will love you, bless you, and multiply you. He will also bless the fruit of your womb and the fruit of your ground, your grain and your wine and your oil, the increase of your herds and the young of your flock, in the land that he swore to your fathers to give you."*

This "love without end" and blessings forevermore are exhibited most fully in the death of Jesus Christ. His is a love far greater than tongue or pen can tell:

The love of God is greater far than tongue or pen can ever tell;
It goes beyond the highest star, and reaches to the lowest hell;
The guilty pair, bowed down with care, God gave His Son to win;
His erring child He reconciled, and pardoned from his sin.[14]

Question 7: What does it do for your heart when you look at the cross and see Jesus pouring out His life unto death for you?

_____

_____

_____

_____

"May the Lord direct your hearts to the love of God and to the steadfastness of Christ." 2 Thessalonians 3:5

---

14   https://hymnary.org/text/the_love_of_god_is_greater_far

The Display of God's Compassion, Kindness, and Mercy

W elcome to our next study of God's character as evidenced by the cross of Jesus Christ. Today, we want to examine the mercy of God as exhibited in the death of Christ.

Let us begin today with a passage of Scripture that illustrates our subject:

"Jesus replied, "A man was going down from Jerusalem to Jericho, and he fell among robbers, who stripped him and beat him and departed, leaving him half dead.³¹ Now by chance a priest was going down that road, and when he saw him he passed by on the other side.³² So likewise a Levite, when he came to the place and saw him, passed by on the other side.³³ But a Samaritan, as he journeyed, came to where he was, and when he saw him, he had compassion.³⁴ He went to him and bound up his wounds, pouring on oil and wine. Then he set him on his own animal and brought him to an inn and took care of him.³⁵ And the next day he took out two denarii and gave them to the innkeeper, saying, 'Take care of him, and whatever more you spend, I will repay you when I come back.'" Luke 10:30-35

Question 1. Please list the specific things the Samaritan did for the injured man that showed compassion, kindness, and mercy.

The story above is an illustration of mercy, compassion, tenderness, and care. The Samaritan *"had compassion"* on the man who was beaten and left for *"half dead."* In contrast to the two other religious people, the Samaritan felt tender pity, compassion, and empathy, and was moved to go and help the man who was in such bad shape. The mercy of God that motivated Jesus to go to the cross can be summed up with the words, *"when He saw him, he had compassion..."*

The one aspect I would like to bring to our attention is that the Samaritan exhibited love for this broken and bruised man not only by bandaging his wounds and pouring on oil and wine but also by paying for his rest in the inn. It cost the Samaritan something to exhibit mercy and compassion in this manner, and this is the picture that is shown to us in the cross of Jesus Christ.

> **Question 2.** How is the Samaritan's payment for the healing of the injured man like the cross of Jesus Christ?

Like the man going down from Jerusalem to Jericho, humanity descended from innocence to sin in Adam. And personally, each one of us has sinned and fallen short of the glory of God. I think of those of my life where gratifying the lusts of my flesh was the norm, where rebelling against God was my way of life. I was involved in pornography and gluttony and drunkenness, and I was in so deep I thought I would never get out. Even if you haven't been involved in any of those things, there still must be recognition of being born into bondage, born into sinful desires and wrong thinking, born into selfish living.

And what happened to us when we descended into sin? Sin *"stripped us, beat us, and left us half dead."* Sin robs us of all good things. It strips us of everything good, right, healthy, and God-honoring. And it leaves us "half dead." Half-dead is an excellent description because, in this condition of sin, we are alive physically but dead spiritually.

And even though religion had no power or desire to save us, but instead passed us by on the other side, Jesus Christ did not pass by. He had compassion for our miserable condition. He was moved with pity, and in mercy, He came to where we were, beaten and bruised by sin, and lying half-dead. He bandaged us with His love and mercy, and as a magnificent display of His amazing grace, He went to the cross and purchased our healing, and our rest, and our forgiveness.

It cost Jesus something to help us in this manner; it cost Him His life. Just like the Samaritan who purchased rest for the bruised man, so Jesus Christ bought our rest in Him and our healing from the wounds of sin, with His very life. Now that is mercy. And it is seen best at the cross.

Next, let us move to an Old Testament illustration that teaches the mercy of God's character, and connects that mercy, again, to the cross of Jesus Christ.

In the Old Testament worship system, there was a covering for the Ark of the Covenant. This covering was actually a "seat" where the High Priest was required to sprinkle blood, once a year, for the forgiveness of the sins of the nation of Israel. The name of this piece of furniture, with the blood sprinkled on it, was called the Mercy Seat. Directly over the mercy seat was the presence of God, dwelling between two Cherubim. As God looked down upon the blood, He would have mercy on His erring children. Please examine these Scriptures:

> *"You shall make a mercy seat of pure gold. Two cubits and a half shall be its length, and a cubit and a half its breadth.[18] And you shall make two cherubim of gold; of hammered work shall you make them, on the two ends of the mercy seat." Exodus 25:17-18*

> *"And you shall put the mercy seat on the top of the ark, and in the ark you shall put the testimony that I shall give you.[22] There I will meet with you, and from above the mercy seat, from between the two cherubim that are on the ark of the testimony, I will speak with you about all that I will give you in commandment for the people of Israel." Exodus 25:21-22*

Question 3. From Exodus 25:22, what two specific things happened at the mercy seat?

_____

_____

_____

_____

From Exodus 25:22, we see that God would "meet with" the high priest and "speak with" him at the mercy seat. Please keep these truths in mind as we read additional verses about the mercy seat:

> "And you shall put it in front of the veil that is above the ark of the testimony, in front of the mercy seat that is above the testimony, where I will meet with you." Exodus 30:6

> "And he shall take some of the blood of the bull and sprinkle it with his finger on the front of the mercy seat on the east side, and in front of the mercy seat he shall sprinkle some of the blood with his finger seven times." Leviticus 16:14

The cross of Jesus Christ is the fulfillment of the "Mercy Seat" of the Old Testament. God looks down upon the death of His Son, Who shed His blood for our forgiveness, and He has mercy on His people. Just as God met with the people and spoke to them from above the mercy seat, so He meets with us at the cross and speaks to us at the cross.

The Words He speaks at the cross are words of mercy. If we linger at the cross and examine it with eyes of faith, here are the words we will hear:

- **Forgiveness:** "To him all the prophets bear witness that everyone who believes in him receives forgiveness of sins through his name" (Acts 10:43).
- **Acceptance:** "_to the praise of the glory of His grace, in which He has made us accepted in the One having been loved_" (Ephesians 1:6 NKJV).

- **Redemption:** "*In him we have redemption through his blood, the forgiveness of our trespasses, according to the riches of his grace*" (Ephesians 1:7).

- **Reconciliation:** "*More than that, we also rejoice in God through our Lord Jesus Christ, through whom we have now received reconciliation*" (Romans 5:11).

- **Peace with God:** "*and through him to reconcile to himself all things, whether on earth or in heaven, making peace by the blood of his cross*" (Colossians 1:20). "*Therefore, since we have been justified by faith, we have peace with God through our Lord Jesus Christ*" (Romans 5:1).

- **Eternal life:** "*For God so loved the world, that he gave his only Son, that whoever believes in him should not perish but have eternal life*" (John 3:16).

Where do we see the correlation between the Mercy Seat and the cross of Jesus Christ? This is an excellent question to ask and is a most enlightening study. Here is a hint that gets us started in this study: notice Romans 3:25, which we studied earlier in these lessons:

> "*...whom God put forward as a propitiation by his blood, to be received by faith. This was to show God's righteousness, because in his divine forbearance he had passed over former sins.*" Romans 3:25

The word "propitiation" (the removal of God's wrath that happened at the cross) is defined this way in Strong's Concordance:

"Neuter of a derivative of G2433; an *expiatory* (place or thing), that is, (concretely) an atoning *victim*, or (specifically) the lid of the Ark (in the Temple):—mercy seat, propitiation."[15]

Here we find that the Greek word for the Mercy Seat, *hilasterion*, is used in the New Testament in reference to the "propitiation", or the cross of Jesus Christ. In fact, the same word translated "propitiation" in Romans 3:25 is actually translated as "Mercy Seat" in Hebrews 9:5:

---

15   https://www.studylight.org/lexicons/greek/2435.html

"Above it were the cherubim of glory overshadowing the mercy seat. Of these things we cannot now speak in detail." Hebrews 9:5

Question 4. Please think through this truth. How is the Mercy Seat in the Old Testament comparable to the cross of Jesus Christ?

_____

_____

_____

_____

What does all this tell us? What is the message here? Just this: the cross of Jesus Christ is the fulfillment of the Mercy Seat of the Old Testament. The cross of Jesus Christ is where God meets with us, where He speaks to us today, where God has mercy on sinners, where sinners can receive forgiveness and a full pardon for their sins, where sinners are accepted and loved and welcomed. God is teaching us that His mercy is most fully expressed at the cross of Jesus Christ.

Hymn writers have found and exulted in the correlation between the Mercy Seat and the cross of Jesus Christ, and have written hymn lyrics like these:

> *Is there a heart o'erbound by sorrow?*
> *Is there a life weighed down by care?*
> *Come to the cross each burden bearing;*
> *All your anxiety leave it there.*[16]

In my past, I lived in many habitual sins, tried everything the world had to offer to break free, but in the end, I could not get the victory. Maybe you have had issues with habitual sin as well. Do you know what I found out in my search to find freedom from habitual sin? I discovered that what I needed was not a new diet, a new pill, a blocker or filter, or a 12-step group, but rather a fresh discovery of God's mercy. What I found out is that God's grace and mercy, when received in the heart, saps the very life out of sin. And God's mercy is best seen at the cross of Jesus Christ.

---

16   https://hymnary.org/text/is_there_a_heart_oerbound_by_sorrow

God's mercy, like the manna given to the Israelites in the wilderness, is new every morning. We must, like those Israelites, rise early and seek it out, feed on it, and enjoy it. As we do that, sin's power is withered, for grace is always stronger than the pull of sin.

> *"The steadfast love of the LORD never ceases; his mercies never come to an end;[23] they are new every morning; great is your faithfulness." Lamentations 3:22-23*

Question 5. Please examine your heart and write out whether or not you are coming to embrace the cross of Jesus Christ more fully through the study of His Word? We do not want to merely gain knowledge, but rather to grow in our application of the cross to our lives. Are you doing this? Please consider, and write out your thoughts:

_____

_____

_____

_____

Ken writes, *"In the past 6 days, I have discovered many truths of how the Cross impacts my life. It is becoming more than just where my Savior died for my sins, it is becoming more of a focal point of God's love and compassion for me."*

Margaret writes, *"Yes, I am coming to embrace the cross of Jesus more fully through this study and also applying it in my life. Although I have known a lot of this stuff, there has been something not quite tying it in. Maybe it has been the journey from my head to my heart that has been missing. But somewhere deep inside, God is fitting the jigsaw pieces together for me and the true meaning of the cross is becoming more alive. During all this, I am drawing closer to Jesus as He is drawing me closer to Him."*

Redemption by Blood

"In him we have redemption through his blood, the for-giveness of our trespasses, according to the riches of his grace," Ephesians 1:7

A few years back, an acquaintance of mine had his car impounded for unpaid parking tickets. My friend was instructed that if he wanted his car back, he had to come to the police station and pay the outstanding parking tickets plus a fine. He said he had never been so humiliated as when he was paying his debt to receive his vehicle back.

The Bible talks a lot about redemption. What is redemption? Why do we, as human beings, need it? How is it accomplished? What are the results of redemption in our lives?

The biblical definition of redemption is the paying of a price to buy something back that the purchaser might regain possession of the property. It is much like my friend, who "redeemed" his car by paying the price. Scripture teaches us that we are God's possession because He created us, but that through Adam's fall, we became captives to sin, under the influence and power of the devil. Because of the fall into sin, we became "children of man" (Genesis 11:5) and "children of the devil" (John 8:44). Redemption for humankind comes by the cross of Jesus Christ, where He redeemed us and bought us back by paying the price. As we are redeemed, and we receive Jesus Christ as Lord and Savior, we are then "given the right to become children of God" (John 1:12). He repurchased us, and as Christians, we are now the children of God again. These are the things we will study for the next three lessons.

Let's begin with a couple of Scriptures that will help us understand the meaning of redemption. In the Old Testament, God set forth a law concerning redeeming the firstborn of both animals and men.

"Every firstborn of a donkey you shall redeem with a lamb, or if you will not redeem it you shall break its neck. Every firstborn of man among your sons you shall redeem." Exodus 13:13

Question 1. What was the price of the donkey's redemption according to Exodus 13:13?

Question 2. What would happen to the donkey if the owner did not redeem it with a lamb?

Under the Mosaic Law, the Israelites were required to redeem every firstborn donkey with a lamb. In other words, they were to pay the price of a lamb to acquire the donkey as their possession. However, if they did not redeem the donkey, then it had to be killed. The teaching to the Israelites was this: it was either redemption or death for the donkey. Either the lamb died to redeem the donkey, or the donkey died.

In the Old Testament command in Exodus 13, God was laying down the ground rules, teaching the requirements, and showing the results of redemption.

Here is another passage that teaches about redemption:

"Everything that opens the womb of all flesh, whether man or beast, which they offer to the LORD, shall be yours. Nevertheless, the

firstborn of man you shall redeem, and the firstborn of unclean animals you shall redeem. [16] *And their redemption price (at a month old you shall redeem them) you shall fix at five shekels in silver, according to the shekel of the sanctuary, which is twenty gerahs." Numbers 18:15-16*

Question 3. What was the "price for redemption" according to Numbers 18:16?

_____

_____

_____

_____

The law pointed forward to and finds its fulfillment in Jesus Christ, the Lamb slain to redeem us from sin. Jesus Christ came to this earth and died on the cross, thereby redeeming us from sin, from an empty life, and our futile ways, by His blood.

> *"knowing that you were redeemed from the futile ways inherited from your forefathers, not with perishable things such as silver or gold, but with the precious blood of Christ, like that of a lamb without blemish or spot." 1 Peter 1:18-19*

But what is the need for our redemption today? Why must we be redeemed, and from what do we need to be redeemed? Please study the following Scriptures and write down what "need" for redemption is listed in each one:

> *"Say therefore to the people of Israel, 'I am the LORD, and I will bring you out from under the burdens of the Egyptians, and I will deliver you from slavery to them, and I will redeem you with an outstretched arm and with great acts of judgment." Exodus 6:6*

Question 4. What need for redemption did the Israelites have as presented in Exodus 6:6?

_____

_____

_____

_____

"In famine he will redeem you from death, and in war from the power of the sword." Job 5:20

Question 5. What need for redemption is presented in Job 5:20?

_____

_____

_____

_____

"Or, 'Deliver me from the adversary's hand'? Or, 'Redeem me from the hand of the ruthless'?" Job 6:23

Question 6. What need for redemption is presented in Job 6:23?

_____

_____

_____

_____

"Redeem Israel, O God, out of all his troubles." Psalm 25:22

Question 7. What need for redemption is presented in Psalm 25:22?

_____

_____

_____

_____

When it comes to redeeming men and women, the Bible makes it clear that no man could accomplish this most important act:

> *"Truly no man can ransom another, or give to God the price of his life," Psalm 49:7*

The Bible states clearly that no money and no man could redeem the life of another man; only God can redeem:

> *"But God will ransom my soul from the power of Sheol, for he will receive me. Selah" Psalm 49:15*

> **Question 8.** What need for redemption is presented in Psalm 49:15?

_____

_____

_____

_____

> *"Redeem me from man's oppression, that I may keep your precepts." Psalm 119:134*

Question 9. What need for redemption is presented in Psalm 119:134?

_____

_____

_____

_____

"And he will redeem Israel from all his iniquities." Psalm 130:8

Question 10. What need for redemption is presented in Psalm 130:8?

_____

_____

_____

_____

"to redeem those who were under the law, so that we might receive adoption as sons." Galatians 4:5

Question 11. What need for redemption is presented in Galatians 4:5?

_____

_____

_____

_____

Redemption is paying the price to acquire or reacquire a piece of property, person, or animal. And redemption for human beings is connected with being purchased out of slavery or bondage, and sin in general. Scripture repeatedly refers to being redeemed from death, disease, trouble, war, oppression, the rule of tyrants and the hand of enemies, the law, and from hell.

In the Old Testament, men and women longed for redemption. They were in bondage under the law, enslaved to numerous enemy nations, had trouble on all sides throughout the history of their nation, and were enslaved to their flesh and to sin (John 8:32-36). They cried out for freedom from their harsh taskmasters, they pled for redemption from oppression, from their troubles, from the hand of their enemies, from death, and hell.

The history of the nation of Israel is a picture of humankind apart from Christ today. Men and women today are mastered by their lusts, enslaved by evil desires, under the burden of sin, in bondage to their flesh, captives of the ruler of darkness. These men and women live lives of quiet desperation, and they cry inside to be set free.

The good news we have as Christians is that God sent His Son to this earth as the Lamb of God to redeem us from our sins. He died on the cross to provide redemption from the power of Satan, from demonic oppression, from the curse of the law, from sin, death, and hell. In Jesus Christ, we find redemption!

> *Christ has for sin atonement made*
> *What a wonderful Savior!*
> *We are redeemed, the price is paid*
> *What a wonderful Savior![17]*

> *"He has delivered us from the domain of darkness and transferred us to the kingdom of his beloved Son,[14] in whom we have redemption, the forgiveness of sins." Colossians 1:13-14*

> *"...he entered once for all into the holy places, not by means of the blood of goats and calves but by means of his own blood, thus securing an eternal redemption." Hebrews 9:12*

---

17   https://hymnary.org/text/christ_has_for_sin_atonement_made

While every other religion in the world teaches men to attempt to redeem themselves by their good works, only Christianity sets forth a completed redemption by the good work Jesus Christ did on the cross. He *"secured an eternal redemption"* with "His own blood." Now from eyes with tears and hearts with gratitude, we sing:

Redeemed, how I love to proclaim it!
Redeemed by the blood of the Lamb;
Redeemed through His infinite mercy,
His child and forever I am.

Redeemed, redeemed,
Redeemed by the blood of the Lamb;
Redeemed, redeemed,
His child and forever I am.

Redeemed, and so happy in Jesus,
No language my rapture can tell;
I know that the light of His presence
With me doth continually dwell.

I think of my blessed Redeemer,
I think of Him all the day long:
I sing, for I cannot be silent;
His love is the theme of my song.[18]

Do you remember your own slavery to sin, self and Satan? I sure do. I look back with tears over a life lived in the flesh, a life lived for my own glory while under the delusion and deception of sin, beset continually by temptation, and covered by shame and guilt. Oh, once we see ourselves in the light, and examine our selfish living while we were under this satanic delusion, our hearts will break and we will weep tears of sorrow and genuine repentance. Then, as we embrace our Redeemer, the Lord Jesus, we will praise God "because

---

18   https://hymnary.org/text/redeemed_how_i_love_to_proclaim_it

SETTING CAPTIVES FREE

He has come and redeemed His people" (Luke 1:68).

Doesn't it break your heart to see the world chasing after the gods of materialism, fashion, entertainment, pornography, alcohol, drugs, food, and a host of others? Oh, how this world needs redemption. Oh, how men and women today need to weep over their captivity to sin and Satan, over their selfish and secretive living. People who are "addicted" to sin do not need step-by-step instruction; they need redemption!

Oh, if I could only give the gift of tears to the moralist who is captive to his pride and supposed self-righteousness, the religionist who is in bondage to tradition and rules, and to poor rich people who may be slaves to their arrogant attitudes and self-dependence. But I can't. Redemption is what is needed. God must redeem men and women from their lack of fearing Him, from their empty lives, their prideful attitudes, their impurity, gluttony, drunkenness, etc.

The Victorian era English preacher, Joseph Parker, once said, "*When God touched my soul into life, I did not call for a Greek grammar, Hebrew lexicon, or volumes of encyclopedias, to find how the thing stood. I believe because 'once I was blind, and now I see.' The heart is sometimes a better interpreter than the understanding. What better proof do I want? 'He has redeemed my life from destruction.'* "[19]

> **Question 12.** Can you say with Pastor Joseph Parker, "He has redeemed my life from destruction."? If yes, from what form of destruction have you been redeemed? If no, please share any thoughts you have.
>
> _____
>
> _____
>
> _____
>
> _____

---

19   https://www.studylight.org/commentaries/tbi/mark-1.html

Redeemed to a New Beginning

*H*ave you ever just wanted to start over? Have you ever longed for a clean slate so you could begin fresh? Have you ever wished you could have a new life where the past is dead and buried, failures are forgotten, and all things are new? This is what redemption accomplishes for those who come to the cross of Christ!

We began our discussion of redemption in lesson 7, and we studied all the various things from which humankind needs to be redeemed. We saw that the word "redeemed" means to be bought back, purchased out of something, or to be delivered from something. Now, please read the following verses, noting from what Christians have been redeemed:

> *"...who gave himself for our sins to deliver us from the present evil age, according to the will of our God and Father," Galatians 1:4*

> *"...who gave himself for us to redeem us from all lawlessness and to purify for himself a people for his own possession who are zealous for good works." Titus 2:14*

> *"...knowing that you were ransomed from the futile ways inherited from your forefathers, not with perishable things such as silver or gold,[19] but with the precious blood of Christ, like that of a lamb without blemish or spot." 1 Peter 1:18-19*

> *"...and from Jesus Christ the faithful witness, the firstborn of the dead, and the ruler of kings on earth. To him who loves us and has freed us from our sins by his blood" Revelation 1:5*

Question 1. Please list one thing from each verse from which we have been redeemed:

_____

_____

_____

_____

It is important to know that whatever truths are taught clearly in the New Testament are illustrated in the Old Testament in story form. Today we want to look at an illustration of redemption from the Old Testament so that we might see this truth more clearly. The saying, "a picture is worth a thousand words," is accurate, and today we will look at a word-picture of redemption.

Let us begin with this passage:

> *"Then came the day of Unleavened Bread, on which the Passover lamb had to be sacrificed.⁸ So Jesus sent Peter and John, saying, "Go and prepare the Passover for us, that we may eat it." Luke 22:7-8*

Question 2. Why do you think Luke includes details about the time of year in his description of the events surrounding the cross? Why, specifically, is it important for us to know that Jesus died "on the day when the Passover lamb had to be sacrificed"?

_____

_____

_____

When reading the gospels, there is never an extraneous phrase or random word added. All have meaning and significance. For instance, Luke tells us about the timing of the death of Jesus Christ, that it was "the day on which the

Passover Lamb had to be sacrificed." This is important, for it tells us that our Lord Jesus Christ was the real "Passover Lamb", of which the Passover lambs in the Old Testament were pictures. The Passover lambs pointed forward to Jesus Christ. When Jesus died on the day when the Passover Lambs had to be sacrificed, He perfectly fulfilled the Law and brought an end to the need for the entire Jewish sacrificial system.

Paul adds to Luke's timing statement the explicit declaration that Jesus Christ is indeed our Passover Lamb:

> *"Your boasting is not good. Do you not know that a little leaven leavens the whole lump?*[7] *Cleanse out the old leaven that you may be a new lump, as you really are unleavened. For Christ, our Passover lamb, has been sacrificed." 1 Corinthians 5:6-7*

Now, with full New Testament authority stating that Jesus Christ died as our Passover Lamb, we can turn to the story in the Old Testament and see how the sacrificial lamb portrayed the death of Jesus Christ, and what this story teaches us about redemption.

Exodus chapters 1-11 describe how Israel had been in slavery to Egypt a long time, and that the Egyptians treated the people of Israel harshly and were ruthless to them:

> *"So they ruthlessly made the people of Israel work as slaves*[14] *and made their lives bitter with hard service, in mortar and brick, and in all kinds of work in the field. In all their work they ruthlessly made them work as slaves." Exodus 1:13-14*

The Israelites had "bitter lives" as slaves. They also had no freedom to worship God or live their lives as they pleased, and they had an evil Pharaoh and harsh taskmasters to deal with every day. Slavery breaks the spirit of a man or woman, and such was the condition of the Israelites' slavery:

> *"Moses spoke thus to the people of Israel, but they did not listen to Moses, because of their broken spirit and harsh slavery." Exodus 6:9*

The slavery of the Israelites to the Egyptians is a picture in story form of the harsh slavery of sin. Jesus connects these two thoughts-sin and slavery-in John 8:34:

> *"They answered him, "We are offspring of Abraham and have never been enslaved to anyone. How is it that you say, 'You will become free'?" Jesus answered them, "Truly, truly, I say to you, everyone who commits sin is a slave to sin." John 8:33-34*

While in the grip of sin, we are slaves to a very harsh taskmaster. If temptation comes, and it does often, we give in, for on our own, we do not have the power to resist. Like the harsh Egyptian taskmasters, sin requires much of us and gives us nothing in return. Sin is a ruthless taskmaster indeed, breaking our spirits through its cruel slavery.

But Israel had been crying out in their slavery, and God cared about His people. He heard their cries and was concerned about their well-being. One of the most definite statements in the Old Testament that points forward to the cross of Jesus Christ is in Exodus 3:8:

> *"...and I have come down to deliver them out of the hand of the Egyptians and to bring them up out of that land to a good and broad land, a land flowing with milk and honey, to the place of the Canaanites, the Hittites, the Amorites, the Periz-zites, the Hivites, and the Jebusites." Exodus 3:8*

Question 3. How is Exodus 3:8 a clear statement that foreshadows the redemptive work of Jesus Christ on the cross?

_____

_____

_____

_____

God "came down" to "deliver" His people and to "bring them up." Here we see the beauty of the cross, where God came down in the Person of His Son to deliver us from slavery to sin and to bring us up out of bondage. This "delivering" from slavery and "bringing us up" out of bondage is a picture of redemption.

But how was this redemption accomplished? What were the means and results of redemption? Let's look at Exodus 12, and we will see these answers, and more importantly, we will see our Lord Jesus in His role as Redeemer, delivering His people from bondage:

> *"The LORD said to Moses and Aaron in the land of Egypt,[2] "This month shall be for you the beginning of months. It shall be the first month of the year for you." Exodus 12:1-2*

Question 4. According to Exodus 12:1-2, what were the Israelites to do with their calendars when they were redeemed from slavery in Egypt?

_____

_____

_____

_____

As God is about to redeem His people, He wants them to know that they are going to restart their calendar year beginning with Passover. The Passover lamb would be slain, the people would leave Egypt, and this would be the beginning of their new life free from bondage.

What an amazing and life-changing truth this is for us today. Freedom from slavery to sin brings a new life to those who were formerly in bondage. Forgiveness and redemption bring about a "beginning of months" for us. When we are released from our sins, it is "the first month" of a new year. Redemption begins a new life! Oh, praise the Lord for the new life that comes from the cross of Jesus Christ as we are redeemed out of slavery to sin!

"Therefore, if anyone is in Christ, he is a new creation. The old has passed away; behold, the new has come." 2 Corinthians 5:17

Many of the great old hymns connected new life with our redemption by the cross as Daniel Whittle did in his hymn *Moment by Moment*:

> *Dying with Jesus, by death reckoned mine;*
> *Living with Jesus, a new life divine;*
> *Looking to Jesus till glory doth shine,*
> *Moment by moment, O Lord, I am Thine.*[20]

"The Lord makes all things new to those whom he delivers from the bondage of Satan, and takes to himself to be his people. The time when he does this is to them the beginning of a new life."[21]

Yes, it is entirely possible to begin again, to have the slate wiped clean, to have a new life in Jesus Christ that is free of the past failures and sins. This is what redemption accomplishes in the life of all who come to the cross for forgiveness.

> **Question 5.** Can you recall the date of your "beginning of months" of your new year? Some people came to the cross when they were young and so can't remember the date of their new birth, others were older when they found new life at the death of Jesus. Or maybe today will be the day that you become a new creation, as you bow your knee to Jesus in submission, and receive Him as Lord, finding forgiveness of sin and new life. How is it with you?

> _____
>
> _____
>
> _____
>
> _____

---

20   https://hymnary.org/text/dying_with_jesus_by_death_reckoned_mine

21   https://www.biblestudytools.com/commentaries/matthew-henry-concise/exodus/12.html

So, we will close right here for today, leaving you with the thought that redemption (forgiveness of sins, release from slavery) brings about the new birth and new life that God requires. In the next lesson, we will study through the rest of the story in Exodus 12.

Question 6. Are you receiving any new insights or new applications from Scripture because of this study? Please share.

_____

_____

_____

_____

Paul writes, *"Absolutely! I have taught children for years, and often felt that the stories of the Old Testament were for lightweights in the faith. Not anymore, as you've so well stated, these are worth 1,000 words as they are pictures of what was to come in Jesus. Thank you for this one incredible insight into God's redemptive plan. I look forward to seeing the entire Old Testament as a photo album of God's people pointing to Jesus."*

Jenna writes, *"It's hard to articulate how this study is growing my faith, my understanding, and my humbling appreciation for God's eternal plan of salvation and His incomprehensible sovereignty over every minute detail. It's just staggering how great our Jesus is!"*

Jesus is Sufficient for Redemption

*H*ow wonderful it is that *"the Lord redeems the life of His servants"* (Psalm 34:22). By His blood, Jesus redeemed us and released us from captivity to the devil, by His power He frees us from slavery to sin.

In lesson 8, we left our study with God's command that the Passover would be the *"beginning of months" for* the Israelite's new year. A new life in Jesus Christ begins with redemption, the purchase of blood.

> *O perfect redemption, the purchase of blood,*
> *To every believer the promise of God;*
> *The vilest offender who truly believes,*
> *That moment from Jesus a pardon receives.*[22]

Now, we move on to more of the word-picture of redemption found in Exodus 12:

> *"Tell all the congregation of Israel that on the tenth day of this month every man shall take a lamb according to their fathers' houses, a lamb for a household.*[4] *And if the household is too small for a lamb, then he and his nearest neighbor shall take according to the number of persons; according to what each can eat you shall make your count for the lamb." Exodus 12:3-4*

Oh, what life there is in God's Word. When we meditate on a passage of Scripture, not only are our minds renewed and our hearts inflamed with love for God, but also

---

22   https://hymnary.org/text/to_god_be_the_glory_great_things_he_hath

our souls become settled in the truth. For instance, the above passage teaches us a fundamental but often overlooked truth in today's world of step-classes, support groups, how-to meetings, etc.—a truth that should settle our hearts and souls in the sufficiency of Christ in the Word of God. The truth is this: Jesus Christ is sufficient!

Notice that the Israelites were to take a lamb for their household, one per family. But if the household was too small for a lamb, then the family could share with their nearest neighbor. Notice that the passage says *"if the household is too small for the lamb,"* never *"if the lamb is too small for the household."* See it? Jesus Christ is "more than enough," always!

This is God's way of teaching us the sufficiency of Christ. He is illustrating here the truth that He teaches plainly in the following Scriptures:

"His divine power has granted to us all things that pertain to life and godliness, through the knowledge of him who called us to his own glory and excellence," 2 Peter 1:3

Question 1. According to 2 Peter 1:3, how much has God given us that is required for life and godliness?

_____

_____

_____

_____

"All Scripture is breathed out by God and profitable for teaching, for reproof, for correction, and for training in righteousness,[17] that the man of God may be complete, equipped for every good work." 2 Timothy 3:16-17

Question 2. According to 2 Timothy 3:16, for what four things is God's Word useful?

_____

_____

Question 3. According to 2 Timothy 3:17, what are the results of the ministry of God's Word in the life of the believer?

_____

_____

_____

_____

"Oh, fear the Lord, you his saints, for those who fear him have no lack![10] The young lions suffer want and hunger; but those who seek the Lord lack no good thing." Psalms 34:9-10

Question 4. Young lions are fierce, cunning, strong, but when food is scarce they go hungry. Yet believers are fed with "bread from heaven", "honey from the rock," and the big and full fruit from the Promised Land (all pictures of Christ). According to Psalm 34:9-10, what do those who seek the Lord lack?

_____

_____

_____

My friend, if we are believers, we must understand and come to know by experience all the resources we have in Jesus Christ. He is sufficient for our every need; He is adequate for all that we require. In Christ, we have *"everything we need for life and godliness"* (2 Peter 1:3); we are *"complete and equipped"* (2 Timothy 3:17) in Him, and we *"lack no good thing"* (Psalm 34:9-10). Jesus

Christ, to us, is what the loaves and fishes were to the multitude-more than enough. *"They ate and were filled. Then they collected seven large baskets of leftover pieces"* (Mark 8:8).

Surely the Israelites, who knew and loved God, were made to understand the sufficiency of the sacrifice when no lamb was ever too small for a house regardless of the size of the family. The lamb was always sufficient for the needs of every member of every house, and if there was more lamb than members of the house, they would share with their neighbor. Oh, the incredible provision of God in the cross of Christ!

Now let us continue our study to complete this picture of redemption:

> *"Your lamb shall be without blemish, a male a year old. You may take it from the sheep or from the goats,[6] and you shall keep it until the fourteenth day of this month, when the whole assembly of the congregation of Israel shall kill their lambs at twilight.[7] Then they shall take some of the blood and put it on the two doorposts and the lintel of the houses in which they eat it.[8] They shall eat the flesh that night, roasted on the fire; with unleavened bread and bitter herbs they shall eat it." Exodus 12:5-8*

Question 5. According to Exodus 12:5, how old was the lamb to be? Keeping in mind that this lamb would have been full-grown and in the "prime of life," what does that teach us about Jesus, our "Passover Lamb"?

_____

_____

_____

_____

> *"Tell all the congregation of Israel that on the tenth day of this month every man shall take a lamb according to their fathers' houses, a lamb for a household." Exodus 12:3*

"...and you shall keep it until the fourteenth day of this month, when the whole assembly of the congregation of Israel shall kill their lambs at twilight." Exodus 12:6

Question 6. How long were the Israelites to keep the lamb separated from the flock? Compare verse 3 with verse 6.

_____

_____

_____

_____

Question 7. Where were they to sprinkle the blood of the lamb? What do you think this "sprinkling" symbolized?

_____

_____

_____

_____

Question 8. What were they to do with the flesh of the sacrifice? What thoughts do you get from this requirement?

_____

_____

_____

Question 9. What does the fire on which the lamb was roasted illustrate for us?

_____

_____

_____

_____

Each of these requirements is designed to teach us about Jesus Christ and gospel truth. The lamb was to be "a year old male," in its prime. Jesus Christ was sacrificed on the cross, not as a babe in Bethlehem but at 33 years old, in the prime of His life. Think of Him going to the cross for you, not as a weak and helpless infant, or an aged and frail old man, but in His prime.

The lamb also had to have no spot or blemish because Jesus Christ was without sin, a perfect offering. Isn't it amazing that the judge who condemned Christ declared Him innocent (Luke 23:14-15)? Jesus was tempted in all ways just as we are, yet was "without sin" (Hebrews 4:15). Think of Jesus' cross, dying as the only perfect Human, trading His life for yours as He became sin for you that you might become the righteousness of God in Him.

The lamb was to be set apart four days before to be examined and declared spotless. Jesus rode into Jerusalem on a donkey, and before He died on the cross, He was examined repeatedly by the religious and governing leaders of the day; Jesus was declared innocent and faultless.

The lamb was to be killed, and roasted with fire, showing us the cross of Jesus Christ and His painful sufferings unto death. The wrath of God is as fire, and Christ was made a curse for us. Think of Jesus willingly consumed for you, giving Himself over to the "fire" of God's wrath out of love for you, dying to save you and set you free from slavery.

The blood of the sacrifice was to be sprinkled on the two doorposts and lintels of their houses. This "sprinkling" teaches us that we must apply the cross to our hearts; we must put faith in this good news, believing and receiving the atonement (Romans 5:11). This principle is why the title of this book is "The Cross Applied," for, without applying it to our hearts, the good news is merely head knowledge. We must not merely assent to the truth of the gospel;

it must grab us and crush us, hurt us, and heal us. This necessary wounding and healing of our hearts comes as we see the Lamb of God (Jesus) dying willingly, loving us unto death, shedding His blood to redeem and rescue us. Are you seeing this even today?

The blood was to be sprinkled on the doorposts, teaching us of the need for others to see our faith in Jesus. The neighbors could see it, all who passed by knew that the home was under the blood and had faith in God's Word. We are not to hide our light under a bushel but rather "let your good deeds shine out for all to see so that everyone will praise your heavenly Father" (Matthew 5:16).

The blood was not to be sprinkled on the entry floor. There is a warning here, telling us not to trample on the blood of Jesus, but rather to count it precious to us (see Hebrews 10:29). We trample on the blood of Jesus if we refuse to turn from sin and put faith in Jesus' sacrifice. Jesus Christ's death on our behalf is precious and costly. The blood that was sprinkled on the doorposts saved the Israelites from the destroying angel, who would not kill where the blood was. This most precious blood of Jesus is our protection from the wrath of God, the curse of the law, condemnation from a Just Judge, and the damnation of hell (Romans 8:1-3).

Now, let us notice a final verse for today's study:

"In this manner, you shall eat it: with your belt fastened, your sandals on your feet, and your staff in your hand. And you shall eat it in haste. It is the LORD's Passover." Exodus 12:11

The Israelites were to eat the lamb with their belt fastened, sandals on their feet, and their staff in hand, in other words, ready to go. There was a reason for this. God was teaching them, and us, this truth: When you feed on the lamb, you will be released from slavery.

Oh, how important this is. Our salvation comes from the death of the Lamb, and our redemption from sin comes as we feed on Christ. We feed on Christ when we receive nourishment from His death. We feed on Christ when we open His Word and sink our teeth into His truth, and we benefit from His death.

"So Jesus said to them, "Truly, truly, I say to you, unless you eat the flesh of the Son of Man and drink his blood, you have no life

in you. 54 Whoever feeds on my flesh and drinks my blood has eternal life, and I will raise him up on the last day. 55 For my flesh is true food, and my blood is true drink." John 6:53-55

Jesus compares Himself with the Passover Lamb, instructing us to eat His flesh and live, which means we are to savor and assimilate Jesus, to nourish our hearts and souls at the cross, and to find life in Jesus' death.

I wonder how it is with you right now. Has the blood of the Lamb redeemed you? Do you know that your redemption is by God's grace, apart from your works? Have you made a public profession of faith in Jesus? Do you feed on the Lamb of God, and are you released from slavery?

Question 10. Is the death that Jesus died becoming more and more precious to you? Are you feeding on it and being released from slavery by it? Please explain:

_____

_____

_____

_____

Jesus Has Saved Us by His Death on the Cross

*A*re you a perfectionist, or do you know someone who is? By perfectionism, we do not mean a good and right striving for mastery (1 Cor. 9:25 KJV), the pressing on toward the goal for the prize of the upward call of God in Christ Jesus (Phil. 3:14), or the striving after holiness that should be a part of every Christian's life (1 Peter 1:16). By the term "perfectionist," we are referring to someone who sets an unreachable high standard for themselves, and usually for others too, and who is not content in life unless they achieve the standard they set. This is perfectionism, and it often makes for miserable people all around.

But there is a biblical answer and solution for perfectionists, which we will examine today as we look at the "Three Tenses of Salvation."

In Scripture, salvation is presented in three tenses: past, present, and future. Please examine the scriptures below and state to which tense of salvation the verses are referring:

> "...he saved us, not because of works done by us in righteousness, but according to his own mercy, by the washing of regeneration and renewal of the Holy Spirit," Titus 3:5

Question 1. To which tense of salvation is Titus 3:5 referring?

_____

_____

_____

_____

In God's eyes, salvation is already accomplished. The phrase "He saved us" is past tense, because He has already achieved the act of our salvation. As believers, we can boldly declare, "I am saved."

> *"...and by which you are being saved, if you hold fast to the word I preached to you- unless you believed in vain." 1 Cor. 15:2*

Question 2. To which tense of salvation is 1 Corinthians 15:2 referring?

_____

_____

_____

_____

Not only were we saved in the past, but we are also "being saved" continuously. This is present tense salvation. For this reason, we can say, "I am being saved."

> *"Since, therefore, we have now been justified by his blood, much more shall we be saved by him from the wrath of God." Romans 5:9*

Question 3. To which tense of salvation is Romans 5:9 referring?

_____

_____

_____

_____

When Romans 5:9 states that we *"shall be saved"* from the wrath of God, it is referring to future tense salvation. There is coming wrath for all who rebel against God, and who refuse to repent (Romans 1:18). Believers will be saved from this coming wrath because, at the cross, Jesus received the full wrath of God on our behalf. For this reason, we can say, "I will be saved."

These are three tenses of salvation: we have been saved (past tense) from the penalty of sin, we are being saved (present tense) from the power of sin, and we will be saved (future tense) from the presence of sin. Today we will focus on the first one, the past tense of salvation. Let's examine some passages:

> *"For the creation was subjected to futility, not willingly, but because of him who subjected it, in hope[21] that the creation itself will be set free from its bondage to decay and obtain the freedom of the glory of the children of God.[22] For we know that the whole creation has been groaning together in the pains of childbirth until now.[23] And not only the creation, but we ourselves, who have the first fruits of the Spirit, groan inwardly as we wait eagerly for adoption as sons, the redemption of our bodies.[24] For in this hope we were saved. Now hope that is seen is not hope. For who hopes for what he sees?[25] But if we hope for what we do not see, we wait for it with patience." Romans 8:20-25*

Question 4. Please write out the verse that refers to "past tense" salvation in this passage.

_____

_____

_____

_____

Romans 8:20-25 sets forth the reality that every human being and all of creation is born into slavery and bondage because we were born in sin. Sin and slavery (bondage) are always connected. *"Everyone who sins is a slave of sin"* (John 8:34).

For many years we longed and yearned for freedom from this slavery. When we heard the gospel, we found hope! The hope that Jesus would set us free from sinful bondage, from slavery to our flesh, from hearts that were deceptive by nature. We had hope that our sins were forgiven through the cross and that through Jesus' death, we could find new life. And in this hope, as we embraced Christ as Lord and Savior, we "were saved" (verse 24).

In our present condition, we are now saved. We are saved from the penalty of sin, which is a broken relationship with God, His condemnation of us as sinners, and an eternity in hell separated from God. But we notice that our bodies are not yet redeemed. We are outwardly wasting away, but we do have the assured promise that our bodies will be redeemed one day.

Let's examine another passage that further expands the meaning of past tense salvation:

> "...even when we were dead in our trespasses, made us alive together with Christ- by grace you have been saved-[6] and raised us up with him and seated us with him in the heavenly places in Christ Jesus,[7] so that in the coming ages he might show the immeasurable riches of his grace in kindness toward us in Christ Jesus.[8] For by grace you have been saved through faith. And this is not your own doing; it is the gift of God," Ephesians 2:5-8

Question 5. How does Ephesians 2:5-8 show the "past tense" of salvation?

_____

_____

_____

_____

Question 6. According to Ephesians 2:5-8, how is salvation described? In other words, how is life different for those who "have been saved" from what it was before?

_____

_____

_____

_____

Twice Ephesians 2:5-8 says, *"you have been saved."* Today we see the salvation of which this passage is speaking is that which gives life to the dead (verse 5). In the next lesson, we will examine how this salvation also raises us out of habitual sin (verses 1-2), enables us to daily overcome the power of the devil (verse 2), and seats us in the heavenly places in Christ Jesus (verse 6). How do we know, then, if we "have been saved"? We "have been saved" if we have been raised from death to life.

In this passage in Ephesians 2, we see that salvation produces a change of heart and life. Those who were immersed in habitual sin ("dead in sins") are now *"alive together with Christ."* Through Jesus' death, we come to life. His cross draws us out of a life of sin, and we now come alive to God. By the truths in this passage, we can see that salvation accomplishes something in our lives; there are measurable results. Oh, how I praise God for this life transformation that flows from the cross.

I remember being enslaved to sin, following my impulses, living in gluttony, laziness, impurity, and drunkenness. All this while I had a profession of faith, but I was truly dead in sins. Then one day, God showed me the cross of Christ, and I saw it with the eyes of faith. As I looked at the cross, I finally saw the extent of my sin and depravity. I saw the love of God for me though I was so unworthy, I saw a way to have life through His death, and freedom from habitual sin through His being bound to the cross for me. God enabled me to embrace that cross, and I came to life (see Matthew 27:52).

Question 7. If you are a Christian, please take a moment and contrast what your life was like when you were *"dead in sins and trespasses"* and what it is like now that you are *"alive with Christ."*

_____

_____

_____

_____

Lonette writes, *"There was a time when I questioned the very existence of God. I lived for myself; I thought I should immediately get whatever I wanted, regardless of the consequences. I drank, lived in sexual immorality, and destroyed friendships. I was convinced that I was free, and others were trapped by their old-fashioned ideas about God and Christianity. I thought I was the enlightened one. Now I look back at that time in my life and shake my head. God has shown His face to me so many times that I can't fathom ever questioning His existence! I have truly found freedom-and because of that freedom, I can enjoy life without the crippling insecurity that used to overwhelm me. I am now a new person who can have caring relationships. Christ is my life."*

From death to life, that is the reality of all who are in Christ, a "past tense" reality that has ongoing effects in our lives.

Now, let us now consider our final passage for this lesson:

"And by that will we have been sanctified through the offering of the body of Jesus Christ once for all.[11] And every priest stands daily at his service, offering repeatedly the same sacrifices, which can never take away sins.[12] But when Christ had offered for all time a single sacrifice for sins, he sat down at the right hand of God,[13] waiting from that time until his enemies should be made a footstool for his feet.[14] For by a single offering he has perfected for all time those who are being sanctified." Hebrews 10:10-14

Question 8. Hebrews 10:12 tells us that after Jesus died on the cross He *"sat down"* at the right hand of God. Comparing Hebrews 10:12 with Hebrews 10:11, what is the contrast with the truth that Jesus *"sat down"* at the right hand of God?

_____

_____

_____

_____

Question 9. Comparing Hebrews 10:12 with Hebrews 10:14, what does the truth that Jesus *"sat down"* at the right hand of God teach us?

_____

_____

_____

_____

Question 10. According to Hebrews 10:14, who has Jesus made perfect for all time?

_____

_____

_____

_____

Ah, now, we come to a most excellent and life-changing truth. Jesus Christ died on the cross, rose from the dead, and then sat down at the right hand of God. He sat down because His work was finished. In contrast to the priests who had to stand day after day offering sacrifices for sin (obviously because no animal sacrifice ever annihilated sin, and therefore had to be repeated over and over), Jesus actually *accomplished* salvation on the cross.

For this reason, the doctrine of transubstantiation (the concept that the bread and wine actually become the body and blood of Christ and not only symbols of them) is an abomination to God. Jesus does not have to continue to die over and over, millions of times, throughout the world. On the cross, Jesus atoned for the sins of His people, brought in everlasting righteousness, stomped on the head of the serpent-devil, and destroyed him through death. He also freed all sin's prisoners who were captive to Satan, purchased eternal life for all who repent and believe the gospel, made us perfect, declared "*It is finished!*" and then sat down. Jesus finished the work He came to do; He has saved us and made us perfect.

The sacrificial system in the Old Testament only succeeded in making sin exceedingly sinful; it never saved anybody. The ocean of animal blood that was shed in the Temple never washed away a drop of human guilt or sin. It never made anybody perfect or holy or separate from sin. But Jesus did.

The life-changing part of this truth is that because Jesus sat down, we don't need to work our way up. What I mean by this is that because Jesus accomplished and completed the work of salvation, we do not need to work and do and put forth the effort to earn our acceptance with God. Jesus Christ's death on the cross *"perfected for all time"* all who are being sanctified (Hebrews 10:14). We can tell if we are of those who have been made *perfect forever* if we are those who are being sanctified (set apart from sin) daily (Hebrews 10:14). Now *this* truth ought to alter the thinking of the perfectionist drastically.

Yes, the "bar" was set high; God's law required complete perfection. And through Jesus' perfect life, He cleared the bar, met all the requirements, and measured up completely. His perfect life earned all the promises of the Old Covenant.

Then, at the cross, there was a great exchange. Jesus took our place and died our death, thereby removing the curse of the law from us (Galatians 3:13). At the cross, Jesus took all our sins on Himself, and He gave us His righteousness perfection. There is no need to strive to *become* perfect because Jesus has made us perfect.

We indeed are to *"work out our own salvation with fear and trembling"* (Philippians 2:12), and we are to *"strive to enter His rest"* (Hebrews 4:11), but these verses must be understood in light of their context. We are to work out our own salvation because it is God Who *works in us* (Philippians 2:13), and we are to strive to enter the rest *of belief* (Hebrews 4:3). In other words, we are to make every effort to believe the gospel and to rest in Jesus' finished work on the cross.

This past tense of salvation, that we *"have been saved,"* that we have been made *"perfect for all time"* is a cause for rejoicing. God sees us through Jesus' blood and righteousness and counts us perfect.

> *"As far as God is concerned, those who believe in Jesus already look just like Jesus—really. Don't laugh! OK, so you're thinking that if this is the case, then somebody up there needs his eyes checked. You see what your life looks like-and it doesn't look like any Jesus you've ever known. That's where the second half of verse 14 comes in: "by one sacrifice Christ has made perfect forever those who are being made holy." It's a wonderful juxtaposition of verb tenses allowing for two perspectives of the same fact. From God's vantage point your transformation is finished. You're perfected—past tense. But from your side, it's a work in process. Present progressive tense. Hebrews pronounces you already perfect with a ways to go. Your experience just hasn't yet caught up to the reality."*[23]

Question 11. What are your final thoughts on the teaching of this day?

_____

_____

_____

_____

Di writes, *"I have already told someone that I had a lot to do today, and I have been in the habit of putting a 'high standard' for myself to achieve. I am never finished or happy with anything*

23   Dr. Daniel Harrel, Park Street Pulpit, Right-Hand Man, Hebrews 10:1-18, http://www.parkstreet.org/

that I do, that's why I am always worn out, because I never sit down and rest. Because of this lesson, my thinking is changing. I know that I have joy, hope, and a future in Christ, but I have daily been placing too high of expectations upon myself as if my life depended on my performance. Now I know I am perfect in Jesus...Praise the Lord! I will rest in Him today, and forever. He has completed my salvation. I will live for Him and not myself by His grace and power. This is a wonderful lesson for me today. Thank you!"

Jesus is Saving Us

*I*n the previous lesson, we learned that salvation can be described as "past tense" in that we *"have been saved"* and *"have been made perfect forever"* by the death of Jesus Christ (Hebrews 10:10-14). We have been saved from judgment, the penalty of sin, the wrath of God, condemnation, and eternity in hell. And we have received the perfect righteousness of Christ, which has made us perfect. We saw that this past tense salvation comes from the cross of Jesus Christ as Jesus died to forgive our sins, as He took the wrath of God on our behalf, and as He was condemned in our place.

Today, we want to consider how salvation is also "present tense" in that we are "being saved" daily. We have not only *"been saved"* from sin's penalty, but we are currently *"being saved"* from sin's power. Oh, how this truth of salvation from the cross of Christ rejoices my heart. I hope it does yours, too.

In lesson 10, we noticed from Ephesians 2:5-8 that we have *"been saved"* from our sins. Now, let us look at that same passage, and a few verses before it, to see that we are also *"being saved"* daily:

> *"And you were dead in the trespasses and sins[2] in which you once walked, following the course of this world, following the prince of the power of the air, the spirit that is now at work in the sons of disobedience-[3] among whom we all once lived in the passions of our flesh, carrying out the desires of the body and the mind, and were by nature children of wrath, like the rest of mankind.[4] But God, being rich in mercy, because of the great love with which he loved us,[5] even when we were dead in our trespasses, made us alive together with Christ- by grace you have been saved-[6] and raised us up with him and seated us with him in the heavenly*

places in Christ Jesus,[7] so that in the coming ages he might show the immeasurable riches of his grace in kindness toward us in Christ Jesus.[8] For by grace you have been saved through faith. And this is not your own doing; it is the gift of God," Ephesians 2:1-8

In lesson 10, we noticed that the salvation of which this passage is speaking is that which gives life to the dead (verse 5). Today, we want to see that we are *"being saved"* from habitual sin (verses 1-2), from *"following the course of this world"* (verse 2), from *"following the prince of the power of the air"* (verse 2), from *"disobedience"* (verse 2), and from gratifying the lusts of the flesh and the desires of the body and mind (verse 3).

The death of Jesus Christ accomplished amazing things and continues to do so. I pray that this study will be a springboard to launch you into a lifetime study of the cross and its results.

For now, let's notice six things from which we are *being saved*, through the cross of Christ, according to Ephesians 2:1-3:

1. Habitual sin: Verses 1 and 2 describe how we were dead in sins and trespasses, *"in which you once walked."* "Walking" is active, moving in a specific direction. In this case, "walking" in sin constitutes ongoing, life-dominating sin. But the Scriptures state that the Ephesians "once walked" in sin, so they had stopped living habitual sin. Something happened, something changed, and they began "walking" and living differently. The rest of the passage describes what happened: they were saved by grace, and they were being saved from habitual sin. What a blessing it is to no longer walk in habitual sin, and this blessing comes directly from the death of Christ on our behalf.

   Question 1. Which way are you walking? Have you changed direction to no longer walk in habitual sin?

   _____

   _____

_____

_____

2. *"Following the course of this world"*: By nature, every person follows the natural course of this world. In other words, we merely drift downstream, floating along with the rest of the world, believing the world's lies, heading toward the world's demise, all the while unconcerned for the condition of our souls or where we will spend eternity. But when confronted with the cross of Jesus Christ, we see that we must alter our course; we must make an about-face. We see from the cross that our present path leads to condemnation, wrath, and death. So, we turn away from our sin, and, as we do, we discover that we are now on the "Way of Holiness" (Isaiah 35:8), no longer following the course of this world. Embracing the cross changes our direction and our destiny.

Question 2. Please consider this truth as it applies to your life. How were you once following along after the course of the world, and how, specifically, are you "being saved" from that destructive course now?

_____

_____

_____

_____

3. *"Following the prince of the power of the air..."* Every person by nature is under the rule and reign and leadership of the devil. We are born captives to his will, his plan, and his purpose. We are slaves. Satan energized us when we lived in disobedience. *"He (Satan) is the spirit at work in the hearts of those who refuse to obey God"* (Ephesians 2:2).

But through the cross, we become mastered by Jesus Christ and come under the powerful influence of grace. We are forgiven of our sins, and we are being saved from the power of the devil. It is not that we can't be tempted, for surely every Christian faces temptation even as Jesus did (Hebrews 4:15), but the cross breaks the power of sin so that we do not have to be dragged into it. Through the cross, we have a new master, Jesus Christ, and a new motivating principle called grace.

Question 3. Who are you following? Are you still captive to the enemy in some ways, or are you captivated by the grace of the Lord Jesus Christ?

_____

_____

_____

_____

4. *"Disobedience"* One of the greatest changes those who take refuge in the protection and power of the cross experience is that of being saved from daily disobedience. When God draws us to the cross of Christ for salvation He gives us a new heart, writes His law on our heart, puts His Spirit within us, and causes us to walk in His ways (Ezekiel 36:25-27). We find that we have a new power at work within us, whereas once the devil was *"at work in the sons of disobedience"* (Ephesians 2:2), now God's Word is *"at work in you who believe"* (1 Thessalonians 2:13).

Question 4. Is your life characterized by a desire to follow and obey Christ, and with the power to actually do so more and more?

_____

_____

_____

_____

5. Gratifying *"the passions of our flesh, carrying out the desires of the body and the mind"* This is depravity. It is following our impulses to satisfy the demands and sinful cravings of our mind and body. The cross teaches us to crucify the lusts of our flesh, not gratify them. *"Those who belong to Christ Jesus have nailed the passions and desires of their sinful nature to his cross and crucified them there"* (Galatians 5:24). Through the power of the cross, we are being saved from "giving in" and instead taught to "resist to the point of shedding blood" (Hebrews 12:4) just as Jesus did.

Question 5. In what specific ways are you now being saved from gratifying the lusts of your flesh?

_____

_____

_____

_____

6. *"By nature children of wrath."* The cross changes our very nature, friend. Instead of children of wrath, we become children of God. Instead of children of darkness, we become children of the light and the day (1 Thessalonians 5:5). The cross puts to death our "old man," our "old nature," our "sin nature." This is why Paul could say, *"I have been crucified with Christ, and I no longer live"* (Galatians 2:20), for the cross had indeed crucified his "old man." Though we still have flesh and so can be tripped up, our old nature is dead, crucified with Christ, and buried in the tomb. Our union with Jesus Christ—His death on the cross and resurrection- has transformed our "natures."

Question 6. Do you understand that the cross produces an actual change in your "nature"? Do you rejoice that by grace you are now a child of God? Are you experiencing the daily benefits of being saved from an old sinful and selfish nature?

_____

_____

_____

_____

"Justification is instantaneous; sanctification is a long growth. Justification is the act of God whereby He takes a man who is dead in trespasses and sins and says, 'I create within you the new life of Christ and now I look upon you and see you just as perfect as I see the Lord Jesus Christ.' Justification is the act of God whereby he declares an ungodly man to be perfect while he is still ungodly. It is as extraordinary a thing as if you were able to say that the caterpillar is really a beautiful butterfly. 'Oh,' you say, 'but it isn't! It still looks like a caterpillar.' Well, that is exactly what God does with us. He comes to us in our "caterpillar status" and declares us to be "butterflies." In reality, that is what happens in nature, too; that caterpillar does become a butterfly. For God has given us this remarkable picture of metamorphosis-that which goes into the cocoon as a worm comes out as a butterfly, for it lives part of its life in one state and part in another. We call this process metamorphosis. It is very interesting to note the Greek word used in Rom.12:2 : 'Be not conformed to this world, but be ye transformed (metamorphosed) by the renewing of your mind.'"[24]

Question 7. Please list out the six things from which we are being saved daily that are mentioned in this lesson:

_____

---

24   2000+ Bible Illustrations, Ibid

_____

_____

_____

God not only saved us once for all at the cross but by the power of that same cross, He saves us daily. Daily we are saved from habitual sin, from the power of Satan, and from gratifying the lusts of our flesh.

A changed life is an indisputable argument. So, when cynics sneer at Christianity and say it is all a lot of nonsense, the best way to refute them is to produce the evidence of a changed life. This is what the cross does; it produces a changed life!

To close today's lesson, please read and meditate on the following passages and take note of how they teach that we are "being saved":

> *"And day by day, attending the temple together and breaking bread in their homes, they received their food with glad and generous hearts,[47] praising God and having favor with all the people. And the Lord added to their number day by day those who were being saved." Acts 2:46-47*

> *"For Christ did not send me to baptize but to preach the gospel, and not with words of eloquent wisdom, lest the cross of Christ be emptied of its power.[18] For the word of the cross is folly to those who are perishing, but to us who are being saved it is the power of God." 1 Corinthians 1:17-18*

> *"Now I would remind you, brothers, of the gospel I preached to you, which you received, in which you stand,[2] and by which you are being saved, if you hold fast to the word I preached to you- unless you believed in vain.[3] For I delivered to you as of first importance what I also received: that Christ died for our sins in accordance with the Scriptures,[4] that he was buried, that he was raised on the third day in accordance with the Scriptures,[5] and that he appeared to Cephas, then to the twelve." 1 Corinthians 15:1-5*

"But thanks be to God, who in Christ always leads us in triumphal procession, and through us spreads the fragrance of the knowledge of him everywhere. [15] *For we are the aroma of Christ to God among those who are being saved and among those who are perishing,* [16] *to one a fragrance from death to death, to the other a fragrance from life to life. Who is sufficient for these things?"* 2 Corinthians 2:14-16*

We will Be Saved by the Cross of Christ

*T*oday's is our final lesson on the "tenses" of salvation. We have already discussed the past and present tenses, that we have "been saved" and that we are "being saved," so, in this lesson, we will look at some verses that show us that we "will be saved." We have been saved from sin's penalty, we are being saved from sin's power, and we will be saved from sin's presence, and all of this is through the death and resurrection of Jesus Christ.

The world (everyone outside of Christ) is without hope. They live lives of quiet despair and have an unspoken sense of doom. Even those who put on a smile and try to laugh away their anguish, experience a nagging feeling of dismay, as well as recurrent thoughts that life is futile.

The reason for this is simple; they are unsure of their future. They know that life is short, and they must admit that they don't know what happens when they die. Therefore they must try to get all the life they can get out of their short years, for they have no hope of anything beyond the grave.

Not so with Christians. We have a sure hope of being saved from God's wrath. We know, based upon the evidence in God's Word, that we will spend eternity in heaven with Christ. We look at the cross of Christ and see our forgiveness, our sin debt paid, death defeated, the power of sin broken, and the devil destroyed. Then we look at the resurrection of Jesus, one of the most witnessed events in history, an event foretold in great detail through prophecies recorded in the Old Testament, and it provides us with a confident hope of a guaranteed future.

As the old hymn says, *"Because He lives, I can face tomorrow,"* whatever tomorrow may bring. In 2020, all believers can say, "Because He lives, I can face the Coronavirus and the associated quarantine and financial crisis!" Christians are realists, but also eternal optimists! We believe we will be saved from the presence of sin, sickness, death, the wrath of God, and every distress through the cross of Christ.

> *"Now, therefore, why are you putting God to the test by placing a yoke on the neck of the disciples that neither our fathers nor we have been able to bear?[11] But we believe that we will be saved through the grace of the Lord Jesus, just as they will." Acts 15:10-11*

Question 1. According to Acts 15:10-11, by what means do we obtain the "future tense" of salvation?

_____

_____

_____

_____

The context of Acts 15 is the "Jerusalem Council" where the apostles gathered to discuss the requirements of salvation (Acts 15:6). Some believing Pharisees were teaching salvation by grace through faith plus obedience to the Law of Moses (Acts 15:5).

Peter arose and addressed the council and made his famous statement, a statement that even today goes against legalists who seek to add law to grace, religionists who attempt to combine tradition and ceremony with grace, and moralists who endeavor to retain the law and minimize grace. Peter said, "*But we believe that we will be saved through the grace of the Lord Jesus, just as they will.*" Peter denounced the law as a means of salvation and called it a "*yoke that neither our fathers nor we have been able to bear.*" In other words, we are saved by grace through faith plus nothing.

Peter taught that, through the cross, God gave grace to all who would believe so that we "*will be saved.*" By grace through faith in Jesus' death on the cross to atone for our sins and His victorious resurrection to give us a new life, we have been, are being, and will be saved. Peter's confidence was in grace alone, the cross of Christ alone, to save all who believe.

I have that same confidence in Christ's finished work. I believe that not only am I saved and being saved, but that I will be saved from God's wrath. I believe I will be saved from the presence of sin through Jesus' sacrifice. I believe I will live forever because Jesus died in my place. Do you?

Oh, friend, Jesus has made our eternity secure and very promising so that we can live with hope, boldness, confidence, and assurance in this life.

> *"but God shows his love for us in that while we were still sinners, Christ died for us.⁹ Since, therefore, we have now been justified by his blood, much more shall we be saved by him from the wrath of God.¹⁰ For if while we were enemies we were reconciled to God by the death of his Son, much more, now that we are reconciled, shall we be saved by his life." Romans 5:8-10*

Question 2. What words are used in Romans 5:8-10 to show the "future tense" of salvation?

_____

_____

_____

_____

Question 3. Please write the three specific words in this passage that refer to the accomplishment of Jesus Christ on the cross.

_____

_____

_____

_____

Romans 5:8-10 is an incredible faith-building text for our study and meditation. It teaches that the cross of Christ is the grounds or basis, not only for *getting* us saved but also for *keeping* us saved. In verse 9, the cross (referenced as "His blood") is the grounds for our justification. Therefore, the cross is the basis for the guarantee that we will be saved from the wrath of God. Romans 5:10 shows that the cross is the grounds for our reconciliation with God. The cross/resurrection event is the basis for the guarantee that we *"will be saved."*

One of my favorite hymns is *There is a Fountain,* which focuses on the redeeming love of Jesus Christ on the cross. The song lyrics progress from the removal of guilt in the first verse, to the washing away of sin in the second, to the promise of the removal of sin entirely in the third.

> *There is a fountain filled with blood drawn from*
> *Emmanuel's veins;*
> *And sinners plunged beneath that flood lose all their guilty stains.*
> *Lose all their guilty stains, lose all their guilty stains;*
> *And sinners plunged beneath that flood lose all their guilty stains.*
>
> *The dying thief rejoiced to see that fountain in his day;*
> *And there have I, though vile as he, washed all my sins away.*
> *Washed all my sins away, washed all my sins away;*
> *And there have I, though vile as he, washed all my sins away.*
>
> *Dear dying Lamb, Thy precious blood shall never lose its power*
> *Till all the ransomed church of God be saved, to sin no more.*
> *Be saved, to sin no more, be saved, to sin no more;*
> *Till all the ransomed church of God be saved, to sin no more.*[25]

The songwriter, William Cowper, had confidence in that fountain *"drawn from Emmanuel's veins"* to remove guilt, to wash all sin away, and to keep us until we are saved to sin no more. Yes, the reality of the cross is that not only have we been saved, not only are we being saved, but all we who believe will be saved to sin no more. We truly can have hope and confidence for living by beholding the results of Jesus' death.

---

25   https://www.hymnal.net/en/hymn/h/1006

In our lives, we face dangers, trials, and hardships. Maybe you have encountered them in the past, or perhaps you are facing some now. You will certainly experience challenges in the future. These difficulties can have a way of obscuring the smiling face of God if we become focused on them. Anxiety and fear can dominate our thoughts; worries and terrors can overtake us if we let them.

If you are facing something difficult, let me encourage you to remember the cross of Jesus Christ and rejoice in your secure and joy-filled eternity purchased for you by your Savior, Jesus Christ! The cross of Christ enables us to rejoice in hope, persevere in tribulation, and be devoted to prayer (Romans 12:12) because, through it, we know we will be saved. We *know* we will be saved not only from sin and its consequences but also from the temporary trials and hardships we face today. Oh, what hope and encouragement this good news gives us!

Look at Jesus' cross. Focus on it. Rejoice in it, even in difficulties and trials, and the hard times that test your faith. Oh, what hope there is in the gospel! And this hope is kept for us in heaven, out of reach of the enemy; it cannot be lost or stolen:

> *"because of the hope laid up for you in heaven. Of this you have heard before in the word of the truth, the gospel," Colossians 1:5*

> *"Through him we have also obtained access by faith into this grace in which we stand, and we rejoice in hope of the glory of God." Romans 5:2*

> *"For in this hope we were saved. Now hope that is seen is not hope. For who hopes for what he sees?[25] But if we hope for what we do not see, we wait for it with patience." Romans 8:24-25*

While the world lives with a quiet sense of dread, Christians live with a burning optimism for the future and hope eternal and secure. Because of the cross of Jesus Christ, *we will be saved!*

Question 4. Do you have a real hope that you will be saved from God's wrath and the presence of sin?

_____

_____

_____

_____

Have hope, dear friend! Hope that, if you are in Christ, you will be saved from God's wrath *through* Him, and you will be saved to enjoy an eternity in heaven *with* Him.

> *"May the God of hope fill you with all joy and peace in believing, so that by the power of the Holy Spirit you may abound in hope."*
> *Romans 15:13*

Question 5. What are your final thoughts on today's lesson? Do you have any questions or comments?

_____

_____

_____

_____

Jake writes, *"This was a good reminder to me. This increased my hope; no matter what situation I am in, I can always look to the cross and know that my future is secure, even when my present life looks bleak. I am glad that I am being continually saved and will be saved to the end."*

Margaret writes, *"Thank you so much for today's lesson; my heart is bursting with hope. My circumstances have not changed,* *but my perspective has. Instead of focusing on the negatives (or what I think are negatives) I praise God that I will spend eternity with Him. It doesn't matter what's happening here on earth....to be there, with Him in heaven is going to be just the very best that it can be....wow!!!"*

The Cross Puts Us To Death

*I*n earlier lessons, we rejoiced that the death of Jesus Christ brings us life. Today, we want to examine how the death of Jesus Christ puts us to death. Our death does not, at first, seem like good news, but as we study, it will become to us sweet and good news indeed.

> *"What shall we say then? Are we to continue in sin that grace may abound?[2] By no means! How can we who died to sin still live in it?[3] Do you not know that all of us who have been baptized into Christ Jesus were baptized into his death?[4] We were buried therefore with him by baptism into death, in order that, just as Christ was raised from the dead by the glory of the Father, we too might walk in newness of life.[5] For if we have been united with him in a death like his, we shall certainly be united with him in a resurrection like his." Romans 6:1-5*

Question 1. What does it mean that Christians "have been united with him in His death"?

_____

_____

_____

_____

Christians have been *"united with Jesus in death."* What this means is that our entire old selfish, sin-loving nature was crucified with Jesus Christ on the cross, and it no longer lives. The death of Christ put to death my old self, my entire past, and my whole identity as a sinner. What a gift!

> *I have been crucified with Christ. It is no longer I who live, but Christ who lives in me. And the life I now live in the flesh I live by faith in the Son of God, who loved me and gave himself for me. Galatians 2:20*

Question 2. Paul was physically alive when he wrote in Galatians 2:20 that he had been crucified with Christ. How can that be?

_____

_____

_____

_____

Paul meant that his old nature, his "old man," the unconverted Paul, was crucified with Christ on the cross. Not only did Jesus Christ die for Paul, but Paul also died in Him. And now Jesus lived in Paul. The same is true for us who believe.

"An old missionary had long lived a defeated Christian life. In his despair, his eyes fell upon the words, "Christ lives in me." "What," he said, "is Christ actually living in me?" He jumped up,—solid Presbyterian though he was,—and danced round and round his table, saying, "Christ lives in me! Christ lives in me!" When he realized that he was actually indwelt by the Crucified One, he came into blessed emancipation from the old self-life.

The life that is identified with Christ will be a life of sufficiency and fullness and victory. While it must not be confused with a life of emotion or of feelings, it is a life filled with "all joy and peace in believing." We must learn not to live in our feelings, for these are often misleading. The Lord Jesus said, "Ye shall know the truth, and the truth shall make you free." [26]

How can we understand this truth that we died with Christ? We can

---

26   Maxwell, L.E., *Born Crucified*, 1945

understand it in the same way the sin of Adam was "imputed" to each one of his children. We were in Adam when he sinned. As our federal head and representative, when Adam sinned, we sinned. In the same manner, Jesus Christ is our Federal Head, our Representative, and when He died, we died in Him.

> *"For as by a man came death, by a man has come also the resurrection of the dead. For as in Adam all die, so also in Christ shall all be made alive." 1 Corinthians 15:21-22*

In earlier lessons, we examined the truth that Romans 5 teaches us about the death of Jesus on our behalf, and of our being justified by faith in Him. Now we move forward into Romans 6 to see the *believer's identification with Christ's death*. In Romans 5, it is Christ's death *for us;* in chapter 6, it is *our death with Christ*. Christ's death for us in chapter 5 is foundational and essential, but it is in chapter 6 where we learn that our justification is not a mere formal or legal transaction (although it is essentially a legal matter), but that it is also an *essential union with Christ*. Christians are those who have really and truly experienced death. We died to sin in Jesus Christ, and are now alive to God.

> *For if we have been united with him in a death like his, we shall certainly be united with him in a resurrection like his. Romans 6:5*

The reason that our death in Christ is such good news is that, among many other things, it provides victory over sin and release from the law.

> *For one who has died has been set free from sin. Romans 6:7*

> *But now we are released from the law, having died to that which held us captive, so that we serve not under the old written code but in the new life of the Spirit. Romans 7:6*

Question 3. My friend, do you see how important the death of Jesus is for us, as well as our death in Him? Can you see that in Christ, we "died to that which held us captive"? Is this a reality in your life?

_____

_____

_____

_____

After grasping this truth of death freeing us from sin and captivity, we can understand how foolish it is to try to overcome sin by using mere techniques, gimmicks, pills, and programs. Sin is much more powerful. Christians do not "recover" from sin; we die, and rise again!

Victory over sin and freedom from captivity requires death! And in Jesus Christ, all who believe have been crucified with Christ and no longer live. In Christ, we have real victory, and it comes through our *death* in Christ.

Please examine the following passage of Scripture, and note the foreshadowing of the cross, and the sinner's identification with the lamb that would die:

> *"The LORD called Moses and spoke to him from the tent of meeting, saying,² "Speak to the people of Israel and say to them, When any one of you brings an offering to the LORD, you shall bring your offering of livestock from the herd or from the flock.³ "If his offering is a burnt offering from the herd, he shall offer a male without blemish. He shall bring it to the entrance of the tent of meeting, that he may be accepted before the LORD.⁴ He shall lay his hand on the head of the burnt offering, and it shall be accepted for him to make atonement for him.⁵ Then he shall kill the bull before the LORD, and Aaron's sons the priests shall bring the blood and throw the blood against the sides of the altar that is at the entrance of the tent of meeting.⁶ Then he shall flay the burnt offering and cut it into pieces,⁷ and the sons of Aaron the priest shall put fire on the altar and arrange wood on the fire.⁸*

And Aaron's sons the priests shall arrange the pieces, the head, and the fat, on the wood that is on the fire on the altar;⁹ but its entrails and its legs he shall wash with water. And the priest shall burn all of it on the altar, as a burnt offering, a food offering with a pleasing aroma to the LORD.¹⁰ "If his gift for a burnt offering is from the flock, from the sheep or goats, he shall bring a male without blemish,¹¹ and he shall kill it on the north side of the altar before the LORD, and Aaron's sons the priests shall throw its blood against the sides of the altar." Leviticus 1:1-11

Question 4. From Leviticus 1:1-11 (specifically verse 4), how does this passage foreshadow Jesus Christ on the cross? What does this teach us about the believer's identification in Him?

_____

_____

_____

_____

As we reflect on this passage, it is helpful to understand the setting and context of Leviticus chapter 1. The Israelites, who God had rescued out of slavery in Egypt, were on their way to the Promised Land. God spoke through Moses to instruct the people how God would interact with them. Every man was required to appear before the Lord at the Tabernacle of worship; however, when the man appeared before the Lord, he was not to come empty-handed: God required him to bring an offering. This offering could not be of the man's own choice but had to be one of the offerings that God Himself had stipulated in the Law. God was teaching them, and us, that the Lord would not accept any man by himself, *apart from a sacrifice.* None of us, by ourselves, is worthy to stand before God. It was the offering that would be accepted as a substitute and atonement.

One of the acceptable offerings was a one-year-old male lamb without any spot or blemish. The man with the lamb offering would come to the gate of the Tabernacle's courtyard, where he would place his hand on the head of the sacrificial lamb, symbolically laying all of his sin and his guilt upon the innocent lamb. When he placed his hand on the head of the lamb, he was not only symbolically laying his sin and guilt on the lamb; he was also identifying with his sacrifice. In essence, he was saying, "I realize that I am guilty, and as such, I should be dying instead of this lamb. God in His grace allows me this substitute, and I am identifying with this lamb in his death." The sinner laying his hand on the head of the lamb, symbolically transferring sin and guilt to the lamb, is an illustration of 2 Corinthians 5:21:

> For our sake he made him to be sin who knew no sin, so that in him we might become the righteousness of God. 2 Cor. 5:21

Because the sinner knew that the wages of his sin were death, he brought the lamb to the north side of the altar and took a knife, slit the lamb's throat, and killed it. The priest would then sprinkle the lamb's blood around the altar. As the lamb burned in flames (symbolizing God's wrath against sin) on the altar, the smoke ascended as a sweet-smelling aroma acceptable to God.

The lamb was an acceptable substitute, an atonement—the lamb's life for the sinner's life.

This man, who knew the true God, also knew that the blood of sheep could not take away his sin in a lasting way. For if the sacrifice truly removed sin, there would be no need to offer additional sacrifices.

> "For since the law has but a shadow of the good things to come instead of the true form of these realities, it can never, by the same sacrifices that are continually offered every year, make perfect those who draw near.[2] Otherwise, would they not have ceased to be offered, since the worshipers, having once been cleansed, would no longer have any consciousness of sin?" Hebrews 10:1-2

Question 5. According to Hebrews 10:1-2, of what was the law a shadow?

_____

_____

The Old Testament saint knew that his offering was only accepted because it was a symbol and sign of his faith in the promise spoken by Abraham that the Lord would provide an effectual sacrifice for *Himself* (Genesis 22:8). The law was a foreshadowing of *"the good things to come,"* that is, Jesus Christ and the blessings that would come from His cross (Hebrews 10:1).

Today we are focusing on the good news that Jesus Christ died for us and that we died in Him. The Old Testament saint, placing his hand on the head of the lamb, was identifying with the sacrifice. He touched it. He identified with it. And all of this is a picture of our own death in our Substitute, Jesus Christ.

For the Christian church, water baptism is symbolic of our identification with Jesus Christ in His death.

> *"Baptism in the name of the triune God (Mt. 28:19) testifies to the believer's faith (Acts 2:38; 8:37-38), symbolizes the washing away of his sins (Acts 22:16), and expresses the believer's identification with Christ in His death, burial, and resurrection and his intention to live a Christ-exalting life (Rom. 6:1-23)."[27]*

I was baptized after my conversion to Christ. When the pastor baptized me, I understood that I was making an outward profession of an inward change of heart. When he lowered me down, I was identifying with Christ in His death, and when he brought me up, I was identifying with Christ in His resurrection. This baptism was an expression of my identity with Jesus Christ, expressing the truth that my sin nature died on the cross with Jesus, and that I was raised a new man in Him.

To summarize, here is what it means to be identified with Christ in His death:

First, it means we participate in all the benefits and accomplishments of His death.

Second, it means His death satisfied all the righteous demands of God the Father: we are personally identified with that accomplishment.

---

27   http://basics.christianuniversity.org/lessons/ST101-03.html

Third, it means His death made full payment for sin so that it is no longer an issue: we are personally identified with that accomplishment.

Fourth, it means that in His death, Jesus took the full brunt of divine wrath once for all: we are personally identified with that accomplishment.

Finally, it means His death struck the final blow to our sin natures, providing entirely adequate salvation from sin and sins: we are personally identified with this accomplishment.

What good news it is indeed that Jesus Christ, by His death and resurrection, brought us not only life but also death—death to the old nature. While Christians still have flesh, the residue of the old nature, causing an ongoing struggle with sin, we no longer have the old nature itself. It died with Christ. Praise God!

Question 6. What are your concluding thoughts/questions about the teaching of this day?

_____

_____

_____

_____

Pamela writes, *"The death of my old nature is an eye-opening adventure... the things that caused me to stumble are more obvious to me than before. Those areas that now would cause me to stumble are fewer, and mostly known to me which helps in the daily battle with sin."*

LESSON 14:

The Cross Gives Us Life

*J*esus Christ died on the cross to give us life, both abundant life here and now, and eternal life in God's presence to come.

> *"Though Christ a thousand times in Bethlehem be born,*
> *If He's not born in thee, thy soul is still forlorn.*
> *The cross on Golgotha will never save thy soul,*
> *The cross in thine own heart alone can make thee whole."*[28]

> *"For God so loved the world, that he gave his only Son, that whoever believes in him should not perish but have eternal life." John 3:16*

> *"The thief comes only to steal and kill and destroy. I came that they may have life and have it abundantly." John 10:10*

Before the work of God's Holy Spirit in our lives, we were *"dead in our trespasses and sins"* (Ephesians 2:1). But God, because of His great love for us, made us alive together with Christ, raised us with Him, and seated us in heavenly places with Him (Ephesians 2:6). The Holy Spirit does this work in our hearts and lives based upon the work that Jesus Christ did on the cross. He gives life to us because Jesus gave His life for us. Jesus became sin for us, died in our place, and now we who have believed in Him will live forever.

When Jesus died on the cross, many miraculous and supernatural things occurred: the world went dark, and the earth shook. The curtain in the Temple separating the Holy Place and the Most Holy Place was torn in two from top

---

28   3rd century, from the German of Angelus Silesius, included in *Masterpieces of Religious Verse*, James Dalton Morrison, ed., New York: Harper & Bros., 1948, p. 148

to bottom. Rocks split open. Many people who were dead and buried came back to life and went into Jerusalem and were seen by many people (Matthew 27: 45-53).

> *"The tombs also were opened. And many bodies of the saints who had fallen asleep were raised,[53] and coming out of the tombs after his resurrection they went into the holy city and appeared to many." Matthew 27:52-53*

It is this last event on which I want to focus, for it is an illustration of the truth we are considering today. The fact that these people came to life when Jesus died is illustrative of why Jesus went to the cross. Jesus died to give us life and to bring us into the New Jerusalem, the city of the redeemed, there to live forever.

1 Thessalonians 4:14 shows the correlation between the death of Jesus and the life He gives to us through it:

> *For since we believe that Jesus died and rose again, even so, through Jesus, God will bring with him those who have fallen asleep. 1 Thessalonians 4:14*

Because Jesus died, we live forever.

2 Corinthians 5:14-17 begins with Jesus' death, and ends with our new life in Him:

> *"For the love of Christ controls us, because we have concluded this: that one has died for all, therefore all have died;[15] and he died for all, that those who live might no longer live for themselves but for him who for their sake died and was raised.[16] From now on, therefore, we regard no one according to the flesh. Even though we once regarded Christ according to the flesh, we regard him thus no longer.[17] Therefore, if anyone is in Christ, he is a new creation. The old has passed away; behold, the new has come." 2 Corinthians 5:14-17*

Question 1. Can you see the connection here between Jesus' death and our new life? Please explain the connection between 2 Corinthians 5:14 and 2 Corinthians 5:17:

_____

_____

_____

_____

The reason that we are a *"new creation"* is that Jesus *"died for all."* When He died on the cross, Jesus poured out His very life's blood unto death, that we who were dead in sins and trespasses might live because of Him.

There is a beautiful illustration of life coming from Jesus' death in the Old Testament in the account of the creation of Eve.

We know from Romans 5:14 that Adam was a type of Jesus Christ:

> *"Yet death reigned from Adam to Moses, even over those whose sinning was not like the transgression of Adam, who was a type of the one who was to come." Romans 5:14*

Question 2. According to Romans 5:14, how is Adam described?

_____

_____

_____

_____

1 Corinthians 15 details many ways in which Adam was a type (or foreshadow) of Christ, and he is very clearly one in the way Eve came to life. Let's read it together:

> *"Then the LORD God said, "It is not good that the man should be alone; I will make him a helper fit for him."*[19] *So out of the ground*

the LORD God formed every beast of the field and every bird of the heavens and brought them to the man to see what he would call them. And whatever the man called every living creature, that was its name.²⁰ The man gave names to all livestock and to the birds of the heavens and to every beast of the field. But for Adam there was not found a helper fit for him.²¹ So the LORD God caused a deep sleep to fall upon the man, and while he slept took one of his ribs and closed up its place with flesh.²² And the rib that the LORD God had taken from the man he made into a woman and brought her to the man.²³ Then the man said, "This at last is bone of my bones and flesh of my flesh; she shall be called Woman, because she was taken out of Man." Genesis 2:18-23

Question 3. Examining Genesis 2:18-23 above, how can we see that Adam was a "type" of Jesus Christ here?

_____

_____

_____

_____

Do you see the beautiful foreshadowing of the work Jesus Christ, the last Adam (1 Corinthians 15:45), would do on our behalf to give us life? Notice the parallels: Adam was placed into a deep sleep, then his side was opened, and out of his opened side, God brought to life Eve. Similarly, Jesus Christ was placed into a deep sleep, the sleep of death, and He had His side opened by the spear of a Roman soldier, that He, too, might have a bride. We note that when the Roman soldier pierced Jesus' side, both blood and water came out (John 19:34), and blood and water speak of forgiveness and cleansing. These are the two things necessary for us believers to have eternal life and to be the bride of Christ.

For we are members of his body, of his flesh, and of his bones. (Ephesians 5:30)

Ephesians 5:30 is a direct reference to the words of Adam when he said, *"she is bone of my bone and flesh of my flesh."* And then Paul quotes from Genesis, and says:

> *For this cause shall a man leave his father and mother, and shall be joined unto his wife, and they two shall be one flesh. This is a great mystery: but I speak concerning Christ and the church (Ephesians 5:31,32).*

Now all is clear. Adam is a picture of the Lord Jesus, who left His Father's house to gain His bride at the price of His own life. Jesus, the last Adam, like the first, was put to sleep to purchase His bride, the church, and Jesus died on the cross and slept in the tomb for three days and three nights. His side too was opened after He had fallen asleep, and from that wounded side, redemption flowed—a Bride was given life.

"The Church, which is His body, was also purchased by the Lord Jesus Christ. It meant His death, asleep for three days and three nights. His side too was opened, and the cleansing water and His justifying blood flowed forth. The Church, like Eve, was a new creation, not by a natural birth, but by a supernatural operation of God, and this "rib" was built into a woman who was to become the helpmeet and bride of the husband."-Mark DeHaan in "The Gospel Guardian."

> *If we confess our sins, he is faithful and just to forgive us our sins and to cleanse us from all unrighteousness. 1 John 1:9*

Question 4. According to 1 John 1:9, what two things happen when we confess our sins? How are these two things related and illustrated by the piercing of Jesus' side, and the blood and water that flowed out of the hole in His side?

SETTING CAPTIVES FREE

God could have made Eve out of the same dust with which He created Adam, but He chose to place Adam into a deep sleep, open his side, and fashion Eve out of his rib. I rejoice that God provided us with this beautiful picture of Jesus Christ, His death on the cross, and the life we receive from it. Meditating on this story in Genesis 2, and comparing it with the event of the cross in John 19, will yield many spiritual blessings.

> **Question 5.** My friend, do you grasp the amazing reality of the cross of Jesus Christ, not merely in an intellectual manner, but as a prize and treasure for your heart? Is your heart stirred with worship? Please share.

_____

_____

_____

_____

If your answer to question 5 was not joy-filled, may I encourage you to go to the cross, spend some time there, take in all the scenery surrounding it, and then fix your eyes on Jesus, Who is suffering and dying under a load of sin and the burden of shame and guilt? Though sinless, Jesus became sin for us, and as such, received the wages of sin, which is death, that we might live now and always. If this does not cause your heart to soar in thanksgiving and worship, spend some time at the cross, looking into the face of Him Who died for you, asking Him to give you the same passion for Him that He has for you so that you can sing....

> *Crown Him the Lord of life, who triumphed over the grave,*
> *And rose victorious in the strife for those He came to save.*
> *His glories now we sing, Who died, and rose on high,*
> *Who died eternal life to bring, and lives that death may die.*[29]

---

29   https://library.timelesstruths.org/music/Crown_Him_with_Many_Crowns/

Question 6. What are your final thoughts about today's teaching?

_____

_____

_____

_____

Jill writes, *"I feel more humbled, and in awe, and in love with God with each new lesson. His Word is so rich, and I appreciate so much the intense focus on Jesus and the cross in these lessons. Thank you!*

The Cross Removes the Curse

"I will sing of my Redeemer,
And His wondrous love to me;
On the cruel cross He suffered,
From the curse to set me free."[30]

My friend, do you realize that we were born cursed? What an awful thing to think about, but what a solemn truth it is. The curse with which we were born is an inherited curse; it comes from our first parents, Adam and Eve. All their children inherited this curse, as did creation itself. The curse is alienation and separation from God, as we will see later in this chapter. How do we know that Adam and Eve brought a curse to all humanity and all of creation?

"For all who rely on works of the law are under a curse; for it is written, "Cursed be everyone who does not abide by all things written in the Book of the Law, and do them." Galatians 3:10

Question 1. What does Galatians 3:10 say is the result for all who do not continue to do all that is in the law?

_____

_____

_____

_____

---

30   https://hymnary.org/text/i_will_sing_of_my_redeemer

Adam and Eve did not continue to do everything God commanded them, but instead, they sinned against Him, perverted their way, and turned to their own devices. Because of their failure to *"continue to do"* all that God commanded, they came under the curse of God, and not only them but the entire earth and all their posterity, and they were banished from the Garden of Eden (Genesis 3:23).

About the creation, Romans 8:22 says this:

> *"For we know that the whole creation has been groaning together in the pains of childbirth until now."* Romans 8:22

Question 2. What is the cause of this "groaning" of all creation?

_____

_____

_____

_____

Directly after Adam and Eve sinned, the Bible records certain "first words", words that were never heard before. Here are a few of them:

- Naked—*"Then the eyes of both were opened, and they knew that they were naked. And they sewed fig leaves together and made themselves loincloths"* (Genesis 3:7)

- Pain—*"To the woman he said, 'I will surely multiply your pain in child-bearing; in pain you shall bring forth children"* (Genesis 3:16).

- Cursed—*"And to Adam he said, 'Because you have listened to the voice of your wife and have eaten of the tree of which I commanded you, 'You shall not eat of it,' cursed is the ground because of you; in pain you shall eat of it all the days of your life;'"* (Genesis 3:17).

- Thorns—*"thorns and thistles it shall bring forth for you; and you shall eat the plants of the field"* (Genesis 3:18).

- Sweat—*"By the sweat of your face you shall eat bread, till you return to the ground, for out of it you were taken; for you are dust, and to dust you shall return"* (Genesis 3:19).

- Sword—*"He drove out the man, and at the east of the garden of Eden he placed the cherubim and a flaming sword that turned every way to guard the way to the tree of life"* (Genesis 3:24).

- Death—*"Thus all the days that Adam lived were 930 years, and he died"* (Genesis 5:5).

These words indicate the extent of the curse that it not only rested on Adam and Eve but also on creation itself.

What a horrible condition we would all be in had God left us under this curse. We would still be under satanic deception, in bondage to sin, under the wrath of God, and would spend our eternity in hell.

The curse under which every person is born is alienation and separation from God. Jesus will speak to those that stand on His left side in the day of His power: "Depart *from Me,* you who are *cursed"* (Matthew 25:41). This alienation from God because of the curse is also taught in the Old Testament. Several illustrations show this:

The first example is the bull killed on the annual Day of Atonement; after its blood was sprinkled on the mercy seat, it had to be taken to a place "outside the camp" (Leviticus 16:27), and there its carcass was to be burned up. The presence of God dwelt at the center of the Israelite camp. The removal of the bull outside the camp symbolized the bull taking the curse and wrath of Almighty God for the people. The bull was removed from God's presence so that the people could remain.

Second, the leper in the Old Testament was a type, or personification, of sin and its curse. Notice the requirement for lepers, as stated in Leviticus 13:46:

> *He shall remain unclean as long as he has the disease. He is unclean. He shall live alone. His dwelling shall be outside the camp. Leviticus 13:46*

The leper was required to be *outside the camp,* away from the presence of God. The curse of sin (symbolized by leprosy) alienates people from God.

How amazing then, that Jesus Christ was the fulfillment of the bull on the Day of Atonement, as He suffered *outside the camp* (see Hebrews 13:12) under the curse of God. Jesus took upon Himself the leprosy of our sin; He bore our curse as He was taken outside the camp to die in our place.

Thankfully, God did not leave us under the curse, but instead sent Jesus Christ to take the full punishment of the curse, that we might receive the full blessing of God:

> *"Christ redeemed us from the curse of the law by becoming a curse for us-for it is written, "Cursed is everyone who is hanged on a tree"-[14] so that in Christ Jesus the blessing of Abraham might come to the Gentiles, so that we might receive the promised Spirit through faith." Galatians 3:13-14*

Question 3. According to Galatians 3, why did Jesus have to die on a cross, rather than receive the traditional Jewish method of capital punishment, stoning?

_____

_____

_____

_____

God taught this truth of the tree and the curse throughout the Old Testament. Here are a couple of examples:

> *"And if a man has committed a crime punishable by death and he is put to death, and you hang him on a tree,[23] his body shall not remain all night on the tree, but you shall bury him the same day, for a hanged man is cursed by God. You shall not defile your land that the LORD your God is giving you for an inheritance. Deuteronomy 21:22-23*

"So Joshua burned Ai and made it forever a heap of ruins, as it is to this day.²⁹ And he hanged the king of Ai on a tree until evening. And at sunset Joshua commanded, and they took his body down from the tree and threw it at the entrance of the gate of the city and raised over it a great heap of stones, which stands there to this day." Joshua 8:28-29

Question 4. What do the above two passages teach about one who is hung on a tree?

_____

_____

_____

_____

These passages teach us that when Jesus was hanged on a tree, He was "cursed by God." He, the Creator, took upon Himself the curse of the creation. He literally "became a curse for us" (Galatians 3:13).

And if we look carefully in the gospels, we will see that Jesus dealt fully with the curse. He took each of the "first words" of sin and fulfilled them, and then obliterated the curse for us:

- Naked: *"And they stripped Him..."* (Matthew 27:28).

- Pain: *"For they persecute him whom you have struck down, and they recount the pain of those you have wounded" (Psalm 69:26). Jesus endured horrible pain and suffering on the cross, that Revelation 21:4 might come to pass: "He will wipe away every tear from their eyes, and death shall be no more, neither shall there be mourning nor crying nor pain anymore, for the former things have passed away."*

- Cursed: *We noted from Galatians 3:13 that Jesus "became a curse for us" for "a hanged man is cursed by God."*

- Thorns: *"and twisting together a crown of thorns, they put it on his head and put a reed in his right hand. And kneeling before him, they mocked him, saying, "Hail, King of the Jews!"* (Matthew 27:29). What deep meaning the crown of thorns has! As He was lifted up on that cross, His *brow encircled with thorns,* Jesus Christ was bearing the curse for us.

- Sweat: "*And being in an agony he prayed more earnestly; and his sweat became like great drops of blood falling down to the ground*" (Luke 22:44).

- Sword: "*But one of the soldiers pierced his side with a spear, and at once there came out blood and water*" (John 19:34). Just like an angel blocked Adam and Eve from entering paradise again by a sword, so the way to paradise was opened up by the sword that shed Jesus' blood. He said to the thief on the cross next to him, "*...today you will be with Me in paradise*" (Luke 23:43).

- Death: "*When the perishable puts on the imperishable, and the mortal puts on immortality, then shall come to pass the saying that is written: "Death is swallowed up in victory." "O death, where is your victory? O death, where is your sting?" The sting of death is sin, and the power of sin is the law. But thanks be to God, who gives us the victory through our Lord Jesus Christ."* (1 Corinthians 15:54-57).

Oh, friend, let's let the realization that Jesus *"became a curse for us"* so that we might enjoy the blessing of God fill up our hearts and souls. Jesus removed the curse *from* us by becoming a curse *for* us, and now we are free from satanic deception, free from sin's bondage, free from the wrath of God, and free from an eternity in hell. At the cross, sin was not pushed away but instead put away. God's claims against us have been fully met. Jesus Christ was forsaken of God for a time that we might enjoy His presence forever. He was forsaken that we might be forgiven. Because God judged sin on the Son, He now accepts the believing sinner *in* the Son.

Oh, what unspeakable joy this brings me even as I write the words. "Joy to the world; the Lord has come!"[31] The hymn writer Isaac Watts understood the blessings which are ours because Jesus took our curse:

---

31 https://hymnary.org/text/joy_to_the_world_the_lord_is_come

No more let sins and sorrows grow,
Nor thorns infest the ground;
He comes to make His blessings flow
Far as the curse is found,
Far as the curse is found,
Far as, far as, the curse is found.

Question 5. What are your thoughts about the lesson today?

_____

_____

_____

_____

Jen writes, *"WOW—amazing connections! I never realized the extent to which Jesus "bore our curse." What a gift!"*

Nina writes, *"Wow. My mind is being blown away with every study. I am so grateful to God that Jesus became a curse for me to remove the curse from me. The wisdom of God is beautiful and majestic, like the greatest poem ever written, the greatest story ever told. Christ crucified most certainly is the power of God."*

The Cross Gives Us Abundant Life

$\mathcal{E}$arlier in our study, we saw that the result of the death of Jesus Christ on the cross was our eternal life. We do not need to die and go to hell to suffer and pay for our sins throughout all eternity. Instead, Jesus' death saved us, and we who believe will live with Him in heaven throughout all eternity.

Today we want to examine the truth that not only are we given eternal life through Jesus' death, but we also receive abundant life.

An obscure singing group called "Mascott" wrote a song called *Bluebirds in Heaven* that voices the longing in the heart of each human being with these words: "*I need more life. I need more love. I've waited so long, the things I've seen, oh, they cannot last...*"

Yes, "*I need more life...*" is the cry of the human heart, and this need can only be met at the cross of Jesus Christ:

> "*The thief comes only to steal and kill and destroy. I came that they may have life and have it abundantly.*" John 10:10

Question 1. In John 10 Jesus tells a parable about a shepherd and his sheep, which has its fulfillment in Christ and His church. The "thief" analogy is a reference to the devil and his work. According to John 10:10, what does the devil come to do to us?

_____

_____

Question 2. Please consider what it means to receive "abundant life" from Jesus and write your thoughts out here:

_____

_____

_____

_____

Strong's Dictionary gives the following for the definition of the word "abundantly":

From G4012 (in the sense of *beyond*); *superabundant* (in quantity) or *superior* (in quality); by implication *excessive*; adverb (with G1537) *violently*; neuter (as noun) *preeminence*:—exceeding abundantly above, more abundantly, advantage, exceedingly, very highly, beyond measure, more, superfluous, vehement [-ly].

Friend, Jesus' purpose for coming, suffering, and dying on the cross, is that we might have a superabundant life, one that is superior in quality, more abundant, and beyond measure.

But how can we understand this concept of "life more abundant" when Christians face trials of many kinds (James 1:2), many tribulations (John 16:33, Revelation 1:9), persecution (2 Timothy 3:12), and are expected to die to our flesh daily (1 Corinthians 15:31)?

The answer is in the reality that the enjoyment of this "superabundant" life is not dependent upon outer circumstances or events, but rather upon our abiding in Jesus Christ (John 15). Tribulation, persecution, and even death can come, but our lives are hidden with Christ in God (Colossians 3:3). As we abide in Jesus during these times, we receive the needed life-giving nourishment from Him so that we may enjoy supernatural life amid these external difficulties.

There is a passage of Scripture that illustrates the reality of the abundant life that Jesus gives quite well, and it is Isaiah 35. Please read through this chapter and then answer the questions below:

"The wilderness and the dry land shall be glad; the desert shall rejoice and blossom like the crocus; it shall blossom abundantly and rejoice with joy and singing. The glory of Lebanon shall be given to it, the majesty of Carmel and Sharon. They shall see the glory of the LORD, the majesty of our God. Strengthen the weak hands, and make firm the feeble knees. Say to those who have an anxious heart, "Be strong; fear not! Behold, your God will come with vengeance, with the recompense of God. He will come and save you." Then the eyes of the blind shall be opened, and the ears of the deaf unstopped; then shall the lame man leap like a deer, and the tongue of the mute sing for joy. For waters break forth in the wilderness, and streams in the desert;[7] the burning sand shall become a pool, and the thirsty ground springs of water; in the haunt of jackals, where they lie down, the grass shall become reeds and rushes. And a highway shall be there, and it shall be called the Way of Holiness; the unclean shall not pass over it. It shall belong to those who walk on the way; even if they are fools, they shall not go astray. No lion shall be there, nor shall any ravenous beast come up on it; they shall not be found there, but the redeemed shall walk there. And the ransomed of the LORD shall return and come to Zion with singing; everlasting joy shall be upon their heads; they shall obtain gladness and joy, and sorrow and sighing shall flee away." Isaiah 35:1-10

Question 3. How is Isaiah 35 a description of the "abundant life" that Jesus Christ came to give us?

_____

_____

_____

_____

Sandeep writes, *"Almost every phrase has the spiritual equivalent in Christ for my life. O, where shall I start?! I would say that the* *wilderness that used to be my life has broken forth with streams of living water that bring my parched soul to life everyday. Although I am a fool still in many spiritual matters, the Way of Holiness belongs to me, and I shall not go astray. Oh, this is the best description of abundant life I have seen so far. Bless the Lord, O my soul!!"*

Isaiah 35 follows on the heels of the promise of great devastation and destruction for Israel's enemies in Isaiah 34. The wrath of God would kill and annihilate all those who contended with Israel, and would leave their nation and kingdom a barren desert. But then God would turn that desert into a place of abundant life and refreshment for God's people.

Isaiah 35 is referring to the work of the Messiah, Who would come to save His people (verse 4). The whole chapter shows the work of the Messiah in salvation and is an excellent description of the "abundant life" that Jesus came to give all who believe. Theologian Matthew Henry wrote this about Isaiah 35:

> *"Judea was prosperous in the days of Hezekiah, but the kingdom of Christ is the great subject intended."* [32]

Let's take a closer look at Isaiah 35 and see Jesus:

> *"The wilderness and the dry land shall be glad; the desert shall rejoice and blossom like the crocus;[2] it shall blossom abundantly and rejoice with joy and singing. The glory of Lebanon shall be given to it, the majesty of Carmel and Sharon. They shall see the glory of the LORD, the majesty of our God." Isaiah 35:1-2*

Salvation begins with a heart that is barren and dry, unfruitful, dead in its sins and trespasses (Ephesians 2:1). But then Jesus comes to it, and in salvation, He makes the desert glad, causing it to rejoice and be fruitful. Singing and rejoicing are always the results of one finding salvation in Jesus Christ. And more importantly, the one who had previously exchanged the glory of God for the

---

32   https://www.biblehub.com/commentaries/mhc/isaiah/35.htm

creation (Romans 1:23) can now, in salvation, see the beauty and majesty of God in the Person of Jesus Christ. 2 Corinthians 3:18 states this clearly:

> *"And we all, with unveiled faces, beholding the glory of the Lord, are being transformed into the same image from one degree of glory to another. For this comes from the Lord who is the Spirit."*
> *2 Corinthians 3:18*

Question 4. How does 2 Corinthians 3:18 compare with Isaiah 35:2?

> *"Strengthen the weak hands, and make firm the feeble knees. Say to those who have an anxious heart, "Be strong; fear not! Behold, your God will come with vengeance, with the recompense of God. He will come and save you." Isaiah 35:3-4*

Out of the cross, flow the blessings of spiritual strength for those who are weak and feeble. Because Jesus died for us, the Holy Spirit indwells all who believe, Christ lives in us, and through His power, we overcome sin, defeat the devil, and live in continual victory (though not in sinless perfection).

The cross also brings with it courage and comfort for those who are anxious at heart. The work of Christ on the cross removes the fear of punishment and provides an acceptable ground whereby we may approach God and ask for help. This knowledge brings comfort and removes fear. To all who are anxious and fearful, the gospel points us to the cross and says, "Behold, your God..." (verse 4).

> *"Then the eyes of the blind shall be opened, and the ears of the*

deaf unstopped; then shall the lame man leap like a deer, and the tongue of the mute sing for joy. For waters break forth in the wilderness, and streams in the desert;" Isaiah 35:5-6

Question 5. What does Isaiah 35:5-6 teach us about the abundant life that Jesus Christ died to give us?

_____

_____

_____

_____

When Jesus walked this earth, He opened the eyes of the blind, made the deaf hear, the lame walk, and the mute speak.

> *"And great crowds came to him, bringing with them the lame, the blind, the crippled, the mute, and many others, and they put them at his feet, and he healed them,[31] so that the crowd wondered, when they saw the mute speaking, the crippled healthy, the lame walking, and the blind seeing. And they glorified the God of Israel."*
> *Matthew 15:30-31*

Jesus also gave "living water" to the Samaritan woman whose soul had become a desert wasteland through sin. Then the *"waters broke forth in the wilderness"* and she ran and told the whole town about Jesus, sharing the living water with them. There were *"streams in the desert of Samaria"* as *"many Samaritans in the town believed in Him because of her testimony"* (John 4:39).

Oh, my friend, it is a miraculous thing that Jesus came to do. By His death, He purchased not only our forgiveness from sins but also our spiritual eyesight and hearing. Jesus healed our spiritual limping, opened our mouths to praise Him, and brought living water to our dry and dead hearts bringing forth joy and rejoicing. Through the cross, He removes our fear of punishment and our dread of both death and judgment; He calms our anxious hearts.

In the next lesson, we will continue in our study of Isaiah 35, but for now, I would like us to consider the reality that all of these blessings listed for us today are a direct result of the cross of Jesus Christ. Jesus poured His life out on the cross and from His death flow all the blessings listed in Isaiah 35.

When we look at the cross in belief, God opens our eyes to see His glory where once we were blind, He opens our ears to hear His truth and to love it, He heals our spiritual legs so that we can walk right and not fall into habitual sin, and He loosens our tongues so that we might sing for joy. He turns barren hearts into fruitful gardens, and sends living water into dry and unfruitful lives, making them glad and giving them joy. The abundant life that Jesus came to give flows from the cross.

Jesus says, *"I have come that you may have life, and have it abundantly"* (John 10:10).

> **Question 6.** Please stop for a moment and consider the truths in Isaiah 35. Is your heart thankful? Do you have a better understanding of the "superabundant" life that Jesus died to provide us? Please share your thoughts on today's lesson.
>
> _____
>
> _____
>
> _____
>
> _____

Geri writes, *"I am in my sixth decade of life, and I have spent over half of that time living in sorrow, discontent, and regret. I have been rejected and felt I did not belong. I have been intimidated by others who seemed to have it all together. I have been abused, oppressed, and depressed, but I am now filled with rejoicing in the splendor of the riches of Christ Jesus, the ecstasy of what He did for me on the cross to liberate me and release me to live the life He intended all along for me to live. I rejoice in His patience, mercy, and grace, His redemption, forgiveness, and restorative transformation—all from the work of the cross upon which Jesus died."*

The Way of Abundant Life

*I*n the previous lesson, we started our study on the abundant life that Jesus came to give us, and we studied the first six verses of Isaiah 35, noting how they depict this abundant life in Christ.

Now, let's continue our study in Isaiah 35, and see new truths about our abundant life in Christ, which flows from His death on the cross:

> *"the burning sand shall become a pool, and the thirsty ground springs of water; in the haunt of jackals, where they lie down, the grass shall become reeds and rushes.⁸ And a highway shall be there, and it shall be called the Way of Holiness; the unclean shall not pass over it. It shall belong to those who walk on the way; even if they are fools, they shall not go astray.⁹ No lion shall be there, nor shall any ravenous beast come up on it; they shall not be found there, but the redeemed shall walk there.¹⁰ And the ransomed of the LORD shall return and come to Zion with singing; everlasting joy shall be upon their heads; they shall obtain gladness and joy, and sorrow and sighing shall flee away." Isaiah 35:7-10*

Question 1. In Isaiah 35:7, what words are used to describe the life without God?

_____

_____

_____

_____

We see from Isaiah 35:7 an accurate description of what happens in salvation. The *"burning sand"* becomes a *"pool,"* and the *"thirsty ground"* becomes *"springs of water."*

The life in sin is a "burning" and "thirsty" experience, without satisfaction. I remember that time in my life, and it was very much like a desert. I turned to impurity, food, alcohol, immoral relationships, and more attempting to quench the burning of my heart and relieve my thirsty spirit. It was a challenging time for me and all who knew me.

> **Question 2.** Can you recall a time when your life could be characterized by "burning thirst," too? If so, please describe it here:
>
> _____
>
> _____
>
> _____
>
> _____

> **Damien writes,** *"My life for over 12 years was a constant thirsting, an eternal parching, and no one could tell me, even if they tried, that porn, stealing, lying, overeating, and whatever else my dark little mind could think of couldn't heal the ache within me. Every day for years, the cycle of destruction continued."*

One of the most beautiful things that happen when someone repents of their sin and turns to Jesus Christ is that they begin experiencing deep soul satisfaction; they find that Christ is the real answer to their deepest yearnings and longings. My life today can be described as satisfied in Jesus and learning to be genuinely content in Him. But it is more than that. God is not only quenching my thirst with Jesus, but He is also enabling me to give grace and truth to others. Truly this former *"burning sand"* is becoming a *"pool"* and the previously *"thirsty ground"* a *"spring of water."*

Referring to the Holy Spirit as a "river of living water," Jesus said this:

"Whoever believes in me, as the Scripture has said, 'Out of his heart will flow rivers of living water.'" John 7:38

Question 3. How does John 7:38 compare with Isaiah 35:7-8?

_____

_____

_____

_____

One of the most exciting things about the crucifixion of Jesus Christ is that Jesus did all He did on the cross in fulfillment of Scripture. We have continually said throughout this study that all the blessings we enjoy in this *"abundant life"* flow from the cross of Jesus Christ. Let's examine how this is true specifically of quenching our thirst and satisfying our soul:

> *After this, Jesus, knowing that all was now finished, said (to fulfill the Scripture), "I thirst." John 19:28*

Jesus Christ, in stating that He was thirsty, fulfilled Psalm 22:15 and Psalm 69:21:

> *"...my strength is dried up like a potsherd, and my tongue sticks to my jaws; you lay me in the dust of death." Psalm 22:15*

> *"They gave me poison for food, and for my thirst they gave me sour wine to drink." Psalm 69:21*

Jesus' body was so dehydrated on the cross that He experienced extreme thirst. However, there is something more in His statement *"I thirst"* than mere physical thirstiness. On the cross Jesus Christ, though sinless and perfect, entered into the state and condition of sinful man(2 Corinthians 5:21). And man's condition in sin can be described as *"thirsty,"* that is, he has unfulfilled longings, unsatisfied cravings, deep heart yearnings. The Rolling Stones summarized man's state in sin with their hit song, (I Can't Get No) Satisfaction. On the cross, with our sins upon Him, Jesus entered into this intense human *"thirst."*

And now that Jesus has poured His life out unto death and risen with healing (Malachi 4:2), we find our life in Him. On the cross, Jesus entered into the human experience of longing to give us spiritual and eternal refreshment. And even more, out of the overflow of our own delighting in Jesus, we have water enough for others. Because Jesus thirsted, we are satisfied and can refresh the hearts of others (see Philemon 1:7). Heart satisfaction and deep contentment and joyful ministry to others: *This* is abundant life indeed! And it comes to us from the cross of Jesus Christ.

One time a missionary in India spoke near a fountain on the subject, "Jesus, the Water of Life." A Muslim interrupted him and said, "Your religion is like this little stream of water, but Islam is like a great ocean!" "Yes," said the missionary, "but there is this difference: When men drink ocean water, they die of thirst. When they drink the water of life which Christ gives, they live forever!" The stream is small, but it can satisfy your thirst. *"He who has the Son has life"* (John 3:36). How true it is, friend; as we drink from the living water that Jesus gives, we are satisfied and experience the abundant life that Jesus purchased for us.

Verse 8-10 of Isaiah 35 tells us that Christians are placed on to a "highway" called "The Way of Holiness" where the impure do not walk:

> *"And a highway shall be there, and it shall be called the Way of Holiness; the unclean shall not pass over it. It shall belong to those who walk on the way; even if they are fools, they shall not go astray.[9] No lion shall be there, nor shall any ravenous beast come up on it; they shall not be found there, but the redeemed shall walk there.[10] And the ransomed of the LORD shall return and come to Zion with singing; everlasting joy shall be upon their heads; they shall obtain gladness and joy, and sorrow and sighing shall flee away." Isaiah 35:8-10*

Question 4. What words are used in Isaiah 35:8-10 to describe the abundant life in Jesus?

_____

_____

_____

_____

The way of the Christian is a highway, friend. It is a clear way and an unambiguous road. It is a *"straight path"* (Proverbs 3:6), a *"level highway"* (Proverbs 15:19), a highway that *"turns aside from evil"* (Proverbs 16:17). On this spiritual highway, God Himself *"instructs us in the way"* (Psalm 25:8). He does this through His Word, which says, *"This is the Way, walk in it"* (Isaiah 30:21).

The Christian highway might also be called *"The Way of Abundant Life"* for we see that on it are the *"ransomed"* and *"redeemed"* who are *"singing,"* experiencing *"everlasting joy,"* and finding that *"sorrow and sighing shall flee away"* (verse 10). The devil's power, also, has been removed from this highway for *"no lion shall be there"* (verse 9). The power of sin, the curse of the law, and the control of the devil have all been conquered at the cross of Jesus, who opened and paved this highway for all who believe.

This holy highway is the *"abundant life"* that Jesus purchased for us when He died on the cross. We could even say that the Highway is Christ Himself, for He is *"the Way, the Truth, and the Life"* (John 14:6), and through Him, we *"obtain access by faith into the grace in which we stand"* (Romans 5:2).

By way of summary, these past two lessons, we have studied the *"abundant life"* that comes through the death of Jesus Christ on our behalf. In these lessons, I have joyfully remembered what Jesus accomplished for me, and my heart has rejoiced in the Lord. I hope yours has too.

If, however, you are weary, burdened, and troubled, may I encourage you to stop and consider the cross? As the old hymn says:

"O soul, are you weary and troubled? No light in the darkness you see? There's light for a look at the Savior, And life more abundant and free!"[33]

If you are one that sees no light in the darkness yet, look to Jesus and find light and life in Him. The abundant life in Jesus awaits you.

Question 5. Considering your own heart, are you finding life in Jesus' death? What are your thoughts? Please share:

_____

_____

_____

_____

Sandy writes, *"For many years I could not understand the concept of "death of self," it sounded gruesome, scary, painful, and difficult because it is. I know; I have walked through it with Jesus. The only thing I regret is that I wasted so many years fearing it and avoiding it. Now I have learned that to die to self is to live in Him, and living in Jesus is life abundant."*

---

33   https://hymnary.org/text/o_soul_are_you_weary_and_troubled

The Cross Gives Us Eternal Life

"For God so loved the world, that he gave his only Son, that whoever believes in him should not perish but have eternal life." John 3:16

One of the greatest gifts that flows from the cross of Jesus Christ to us is eternal life.

"Whoever believes in the Son has eternal life; whoever does not obey the Son shall not see life, but the wrath of God remains on him." John 3:36

Question 1. According to John 3:36 above, what is the condition of those who do not believe and obey Jesus Christ?

_____

_____

_____

Because we know our sins were against God, Who is eternal, the punishment for them should be eternal as well. Our sin is worthy of hell. And indeed, there is a lake of fire awaiting those who die, refusing to believe in Christ. God's wrath remains on them throughout all eternity. While believers have endless hope, unbelievers have a hopeless end.

God has demonstrated His wrath against wickedness in various ways throughout history. God destroyed the world by flood in Noah's day. He executed judgment on Pharaoh and the nation of Egypt when He took the life of every firstborn son and then buried Pharaoh and his officers alive in the Red Sea. Later God rained down fire and brimstone on Sodom and Gomorrah for their unrelenting wickedness. And these stories of God pouring out His wrath on unbelievers are examples for all who will not repent and believe today:

> *"...just as Sodom and Gomorrah and the surrounding cities, which likewise indulged in sexual immorality and pursued unnatural desire, serve as an example by undergoing a punishment of eternal fire." Jude 1:7*

The "eternal fire" is the destination of all who will not turn from sin and embrace Jesus Christ.

Someone may say, "you're just preaching that old hell-fire and brimstone message, trying to scare me into becoming a Christian."

The *"eternal fire"* is the destination of all who will not turn from sin and embrace Jesus Christ.

Some unbelievers may say, "You're just preaching that old hell-fire and brimstone message, trying to scare me into becoming a Christian." My response is that if you are not a Christian, you *should* be scared; in fact, you should be terrified.

Consider the destruction of Sodom and Gomorrah and see in it the "example" of the *eternal* future of all who refuse Christ. Look at the cross where God poured out His wrath on His own Son Jesus, and see the hatred of God against sin and know that unbelievers will face that wrath if they do not take shelter in Jesus. The day is coming when unbelievers will flee to the mountains and beg the rocks to fall on them to hide them from the wrath of the Lamb, for it would be much preferred to be smashed and killed by a natural disaster than to face God's wrath. And yet the reality is that even if unbelievers *could* be killed by the rocks falling on them, they would *still* have to face the wrath of the Lamb, for *"it is appointed for man to die once and then the judgment"* (Hebrews 9:27).

"Then the kings of the earth and the great ones and the generals and the rich and the powerful, and everyone, slave and free, hid themselves in the caves and among the rocks of the mountains,[16] calling to the mountains and rocks, "Fall on us and hide us from the face of him who is seated on the throne, and from the wrath of the Lamb." Revelation 6:15-16

It is so challenging for me to write these words, and I do so with a broken heart and tears in my eyes, but if we refuse God's grace and the gift of eternal life, our future, our *eternal* future, is horrible. We will be separated from God and cast into eternal flames.

But the good news is that on the cross, God saw fit to transfer the sins of all who do believe, to His Son. God chose to accept Jesus' death in our place as full payment for the sins of all who repent and believe. And for all who are now in Christ by faith, there is no more wrath of God left for us for God exhausted it all at the cross. Now, it is a most comforting and stabilizing and joy-producing truth, to know that when Jesus died on the cross, He paid our debt of sin and secured our eternal life with Him.

So not only did Jesus' death put us to death in Him and bring us abundant life, as we have noted in the previous lessons, but it also brought us eternal life.

Let us examine some Scriptures that teach this:

"But now that you have been set free from sin and have become slaves of God, the fruit you get leads to sanctification and its end, eternal life.[23] For the wages of sin is death, but the free gift of God is eternal life in Christ Jesus our Lord." Romans 6:22-23

Question 2. According to Romans 6:22, what change had happened in the life of those to whom Paul was writing?

_____

_____

_____

_____

Question 3. In Romans 6:23, what is death called? What is eternal life called?

_____

_____

_____

_____

In Romans 6, Paul is writing to believers who had undergone quite a change. They had been set free from habitual sin and had become slaves of God; they experienced repentance. Repentance is turning our backs on sin, turning toward the Lord, and becoming captive to Him, and repentance leads to eternal life.

But Romans 6:23 tells us that eternal life is a gift of God so we can understand that we do the repenting and God does the giving. The Romans repented, were set free from sin by God's grace, and received the miraculous gift of eternal life. 2 Timothy 2:25-26 confirms that repentance is a gift given sovereignly by Almighty God. How gracious of God to turn these Romans from their sin to His Son, and grant eternal life to them.

We also notice in Romans 6:23 that death is "the wages of sin." Wages are not given as a gift, but rather as that which is rightfully due. Because all have sinned, all are legally owed the wages of their sin, which is death. But instead, God gave the wages of our sin to His Son, though Christ had not earned them, that He might give the gift of eternal life to all who believe.

"that whoever believes in him may have eternal life." John 3:15

"For this is the will of my Father, that everyone who looks on the Son and believes in him should have eternal life, and I will raise him up on the last day." John 6:40

"Truly, truly, I say to you, whoever believes has eternal life." John 6:47

"But I received mercy for this reason, that in me, as the foremost, Jesus Christ might display his perfect patience as an example to those who were to believe in him for eternal life." 1 Timothy 1:16

Question 4. Earlier we saw from the book of Jude that the fire which destroyed Sodom and Gomorrah was an "example" for all who refused to repent and believe. In 1 Timothy 1:16, we see that Paul is also an example. Of what and to whom is Paul an example?

_____

_____

_____

_____

Paul is an example of God's patience and grace for all who will believe. Maybe some say in their hearts, "my sins are too bad, I've been in them too long, and there is no hope for me." Oh no, look at Paul, formerly Saul, who persecuted God's people and put them to death, and then see the amazing grace which transformed Paul's heart and life. Let this miraculous transforming work of God's grace give you hope! God changed a terrorist into an evangelist, a persecutor of the church into a preacher of the gospel; He can transform your heart and life as well.

Believe that in turning to Jesus, there will be plenty of grace, your sins will be forgiven, and you will receive eternal life as a gift. And through believing, you may *know* that you have eternal life.

"I write these things to you who believe in the name of the Son of God that you may know that you have eternal life." 1 John 5:13

Yes, friend, one of the greatest blessings flowing from the cross of Jesus Christ is our eternal life. For believers, death and hell were swallowed up at the cross, and life and eternity were purchased on our behalf. We need no other refuge. Oh, rejoice with me in the cross! In Jesus, we have eternal life:

"Simon Peter answered him, "Lord, to whom shall we go? You have the words of eternal life," John 6:68

Pliny the Elder was a Roman writer who lived during the same time as Jesus. He recorded the account of the setting of a massive obelisk, which, when erect, would stand 99 feet tall. Twenty-thousand workers were chosen to pull on the ropes and activate the hoisting apparatus. The operation was one of great responsibility and risk. Just one error could cause the obelisk to fall, ruining years of work. To ensure the complete attention and best direction of the engineer in charge of placing the pillar, the King ordered the engineer's own son to be strapped to the apex of it so that the engineer's heart, as well as his head, would be given to the task.

One day on Calvary, God's only begotten Son, Jesus was raised on a cross before a sinful, jeering crowd, as the Father watched intently from heaven. God's heart and mind were on His Son that day. There, Jesus hung in death so that we might have eternal life. God has firmly established His Church through the raising of His Son; and we have eternal life through Jesus' death on the cross!

Question 5. How are you doing today? What are your thoughts on this lesson?

_____

_____

_____

_____

Ralph writes, *"I am doing great today. Jesus' death put us to death in Him, brings us life, and brings us abundant life, but it also brought us eternal life. Let anyone who is thirsty come to Jesus and drink. The rivers of living water will flow from the heart of those who believe in Jesus Christ."*

The Cross Provides
Victory Over Sin

We have mentioned in previous lessons that the cross of Jesus Christ crucified not only our sin but also put our entire old nature to death. Death is separation; physical death separates the body from the soul. When Jesus died on the cross, He separated us from our sins, and also from our old nature, which is why Paul could say, "*I have been crucified with Christ, and I no longer live...*" (Galatians 2:20).

Today we want to see that the cross is the foundation or the basis for our victory over sin. Oh, what blessings are ours through the cross of Jesus Christ. As the great refrain of the hymn *Victory in Jesus* says so clearly, "He plunged us to *victory beneath the cleansing flood.*"

Let us now examine both the first and last parts of 1 Corinthians chapter 15, noting that this passage begins with the gospel of Jesus Christ, which is of "first importance," and ends with "victory":

> "*Now I would remind you, brothers, of the gospel I preached to you, which you received, in which you stand, and by which you are being saved, if you hold fast to the word I preached to you- unless you believed in vain. For I delivered to you as of first importance what I also received: that Christ died for our sins in accordance with the Scriptures, that he was buried, that he was raised on the third day in accordance with the Scriptures, and that he appeared to Cephas, then to the twelve. Then he appeared to more than five hundred brothers at one time, most of whom are still alive, though some have fallen asleep." 1 Corinthians 15:1-6*

"When the perishable puts on the imperishable, and the mortal puts on immortality, then shall come to pass the saying that is written: "Death is swallowed up in victory." "O death, where is your victory? O death, where is your sting?" The sting of death is sin, and the power of sin is the law. But thanks be to God, who gives us the victory through our Lord Jesus Christ. Therefore, my beloved brothers, be steadfast, immovable, always abounding in the work of the Lord, knowing that in the Lord your labor is not in vain." 1 Corinthians 15:54-58

In the first four verses of 1 Corinthians 15, Paul reminds the Corinthians of the gospel, which he says is of *"first importance."* This gospel is made up of two parts and contains two proofs.

> **Question 1.** According to 1 Corinthians 15:3-4, what are the two parts of the gospel?
>
> _____
>
> _____
>
> _____
>
> _____

The two parts of the gospel are:

1. *"Christ died for our sins in accordance with the Scriptures."*

2. *"He was raised on the third day in accordance with the Scriptures."*

The two proofs are:

1. *"He was buried."*

2. *"He appeared to Cephas, then to the twelve. Then He appeared to more than five hundred brothers at one time..."*

SETTING CAPTIVES FREE

In the middle section of 1 Corinthians 15, Paul discourses on the resurrection, both of Jesus Christ and all believers.

Finally, at the end of the chapter, Paul applies the gospel, revealing that the result of the gospel is victory over all our enemies, including the final enemy of death itself. The gospel is the grounds and basis for our victory over all enemies. We will live forever because Jesus died for us and rose again.

> **Question 2.** Paul said this gospel of the death and resurrection of Jesus is "*according to the Scriptures*" (1 Corinthians 15:3-4). To what Scriptures is Paul referring?
> ☐ The New Testament
> ☐ The Gospels
> ☐ The Old Testament

When Paul said that the gospel was "*according to the Scriptures*," he was referring to the Old Testament Scriptures. There are many places where the Old Testament Scriptures speak to us about victory through the cross of Jesus Christ. Let's consider a few today.

One Old Testament reference to victory through the cross is Genesis 3:15:

> "*I will put enmity between you and the woman, and between your offspring and her offspring; he shall bruise your head, and you shall bruise his heel.*" Genesis 3:15

> **Question 3.** How does Genesis 3:15 point forward to the coming Messiah and show the victory promised us through Him?
>
> _____
>
> _____
>
> _____
>
> _____

The picture in Genesis 3:15 is that of the Promised One stepping on the head of the serpent to kill him. While he is crushing the snake, the Messiah would be "bruised," but through His bruising, He would be triumphant, and free those who were in bondage to the serpent's deceptive temptations. This battle happened at the cross of Jesus Christ, where He was *"bruised for our iniquities"* (Isaiah 53:5) while defeating the devil (Hebrews 2:14). There is victory at the cross of Jesus for all who believe!

Another famous passage that is one of the most precise prophecies of the cross of Jesus Christ in the Old Testament, Isaiah 53, ends with this verse:

> *"Therefore I will divide him a portion with the many, and he shall divide the spoil with the strong, because he poured out his soul to death and was numbered with the transgressors; yet he bore the sin of many, and makes intercession for the transgressors."*
> *Isaiah 53:12*

Question 4. How does Isaiah 53:12 speak of the victory Jesus won on the cross?

_____

_____

_____

_____

Isaiah 53:12 speaks of victory. It speaks of *"dividing the spoil,"* which is a military term indicating a great conquest and triumph, and the ensuing enjoyment of the "spoil" of the battle. The basis for *"dividing the spoil"* in victory is that Jesus Christ was *"wounded for our transgressions," "bruised for our iniquities"* (verse 5) and was *"cut off from the land of the living"* when His Father *"crushed Him," "put Him to grief"* and *"made His soul an offering for sin"* (verse 10) on the cross.

Do you see and understand how important this subject is? Our victory over sin is directly related to what Jesus Christ did on the cross. When Jesus died, He both purchased our forgiveness and broke the power of sin.

I lived in grave, disgusting, and deceptive sin for many years. The *O Holy*

Night lyric "long lay the world, in sin and error, pining" were right about me. But then something happened. "He appeared!" My eyes were turned toward the cross, and there I found both forgiveness for and freedom from my sins.

Yes, all of this victory and freedom happens at the cross. Sin and Satan are defeated; guilt and shame are removed. There is victory through the cross of Jesus!

Remember that whatever is taught in the New Testament is vividly illustrated in the Old Testament in story form. Today, and the following two days, we will examine some of these illustrations of victory through the cross.

The first Old Testament illustration we will consider is Exodus 17:8-13:

> *"Then Amalek came and fought with Israel at Rephidim.⁹ So Moses said to Joshua, "Choose for us men, and go out and fight with Amalek. Tomorrow I will stand on the top of the hill with the staff of God in my hand."¹⁰ So Joshua did as Moses told him, and fought with Amalek, while Moses, Aaron, and Hur went up to the top of the hill.¹¹ Whenever Moses held up his hand, Israel prevailed, and whenever he lowered his hand, Amalek prevailed.¹² But Moses' hands grew weary, so they took a stone and put it under him, and he sat on it, while Aaron and Hur held up his hands, one on one side, and the other on the other side. So his hands were steady until the going down of the sun.¹³ And Joshua overwhelmed Amalek and his people with the sword." Exodus 17:8-13*

Question 5. How does Exodus 17:8-13 depict victory at the cross?

_____

_____

_____

_____

Here we see the newly liberated Israelites facing one of their first battles as freed people. And God had some things to teach His people, the main lesson being that though they were to fight, the battle was the Lord's, and the outcome was up to Him.

For this reason, while Joshua took the fighting men into battle, Moses took two men, Aaron and Hur, to the top of a hill, to intercede on behalf of God's people. And as long as Moses' arms were up, the Israelites won, when Moses dropped his arms, their enemies gained the upper hand. The outcome of the battle was that *"Joshua overwhelmed Amalek and his people with the sword."* Wow! What an extraordinary way to win the war, right?

Are you wondering how this story applies to us? Or how it points to the cross and the victory we receive through it?

Well, first, we can see that, though Joshua and all the soldiers did the fighting, the battle was truly won by what Moses did on the hill. Exodus 17:11 said that when Moses held up his hands, Israel prevailed, but when Moses lowered his hands, Amalek prevailed. So even though Joshua and his troops were engaged in combat, God made the outcome of the battle dependent on Moses' intercession.

Secondly, we see that Moses took two other men to the top of the hill with him, so that there would be three men on the hill, but the one in the center won the battle for his soldiers below. The victory was won by what that one man did on the hill. Do you see Jesus now?

Now we can start to understand some critical things about this battle account and how it applies to us. Every day, we are like the Israelites, fighting the battle against sin, against wrong desires, against temptation, against the deceitful scheming of the devil.

But how do we fight against the devil, against wrong thoughts and actions, against selfish motives, against our very selves?

Well, can you picture this with me for just a moment? Joshua and the troops are fighting the Amalekites to death. They are in the heat of the battle; spears are clanging, blood is flying, people are dying. And just then, an Israelite soldier turns to a hill in the distance and catches a glimpse of three men on that hill, and the man in the center has his arms outstretched and upraised in victory. He understands that it is Moses, and he is interceding on their behalf and is praying for them.

Oh, friend, two thousand years ago, on a hill far away, three men were hanging on crosses. The Man in the middle had ascended the hill with his cross to fight a crucial battle, not for Himself but for us. He went to fight the devil (Hebrews 2:14) and win for us.

Similar to how the Israelite victory was won by what Moses did on the hill in Joshua's day, our battles are won by what that Man (Jesus) did on the hill of Calvary. Jesus Christ held out His arms and died on the hill of Calvary, but by His death, He defeated the devil and crucified our sin. His cross was a sword plunged into the heart of our enemy. Jesus defeated the devil's accusations against us, for what can the devil say about one whose sins have been washed away? He defeated the devil's power, for the devil's power consists in deception, and now the whole world sees that the devil's intention is not to give life but rather to kill. On the cross, as Jesus' arms were outstretched and upraised in victory, He won the battle for us.

My friend, do you struggle with the power of temptation and sin? Look to Jesus! Do you find yourself falling and receiving wounds at the hands of your enemy? Look up and see the Man, Jesus on the hill interceding for you, defeating the devil on your behalf, securing your full pardon, and victory over sin. The battle will not be won by your efforts, but by the work of Another. Your victory is in Jesus' death on the cross.

As we catch sight of the horror of that cross, the torture of that innocent and pure Man, of the blood He shed for our forgiveness and reconciliation, we are strengthened to fight, and energized for success in the battle.

When the battle was over, Joshua could have said as we can today, *"thanks be to God, who gives us the victory"* through that man on the hill (*1 Corinthians 15:57*); truly, *"I can do all things through Christ Who strengthens me."* (*Philippians 4:13*)

Question 6. Are you thankful for the cross? Do you see how God used it to bring you victory? What are your thoughts?

_____

_____

_____

_____

Richard writes, *"It is amazing how the Scriptures come alive in this Bible study. Through my years of being a Christian, I have* *always concentrated on the New Testament, as I thought that that was all that applied to me. I was missing so much by not studying the Old Testament, it amazes me how much it reveals the character of Christ, how it points to Christ. I have noticed since I began this Bible study, how everything in the Bible has an arrow on it pointing directly to one single event, the death and resurrection of Christ. That is so cool!! It also reiterates how important that one single event is. Without it, there would be no point to any of it."*

LESSON 20:

The Cross Provides Victory and Freedom

One stanza of Martin Luther's hymn **A Mighty Fortress is our God** sets the stage for today's ongoing examination of the victory we have in Jesus Christ:

> *"Did we in our own strength confide, our*
> *striving would be losing;*
> *Were not the right Man on our side, the Man of*
> *God's own choosing:*
> *Dost ask who that may be? Christ Jesus, it is He;*
> *Lord Sabaoth, His Name, from age to*
> *age the same,*
> *And He must win the battle."*[34]

Question 1. This verse of the hymn A Mighty Fortress is our God teaches us two particularly important truths. What are they?

_____

_____

_____

_____

---

34   https://hymnary.org/text/a_mighty_fortress_is_our_god_a_bulwark

The hymn teaches us two essential truths: our inability to save ourselves and Christ's ability to save us. It states that striving in our own strength is losing, but Jesus Christ wins the battle for us. Martin Luther knew the horrible weakness of the flesh, as well as how to depend upon Jesus for victory. He understood that the way to lose the battle would be to trust in his own strength because Jesus Christ alone must *"win the battle."* Dr. Luther was singing the truth found in 1 Samuel 17:47 and Zechariah 4:6:

> *"...and that all this assembly may know that the LORD saves not with sword and spear. For the battle is the LORD's, and he will give you into our hand." 1 Samuel 17:47*

> *"Then he said to me, "This is the word of the LORD to Zerubbabel: Not by might, nor by power, but by my Spirit, says the LORD of hosts." Zechariah 4:6*

For years I attempted to fight in my own strength and only met with defeat. I tried to overpower an enemy much more potent than I and received many wounds at his hands for my efforts. I tried to subdue my flesh by my own "might and power," and in the end, I believed I would never win the battle over sin, self, and Satan. And I still haven't. But Jesus has! He came to me as conquering King and won my heart. Jesus defeated the power of Satan and subdued my rebellious flesh. In every believer's heart and life, "He must win the battle." Yes, Jesus wins; He must!

Some say "a picture is worth a thousand words", and God gives us many pictures of the cross in the Old Testament. One of the most vivid images of victory at the cross is recorded for us in Judges 16.

> *"Samson went to Gaza, and there he saw a prostitute, and he went in to her.[2] The Gazites were told, "Samson has come here." And they surrounded the place and set an ambush for him all night at the gate of the city. They kept quiet all night, saying, "Let us wait till the light of the morning; then we will kill him."[3] But Samson lay till midnight, and at midnight he arose and took hold of the doors of the gate of the city and the two posts, and pulled them*

up, bar and all, and put them on his shoulders and carried them
to the top of the hill that is in front of Hebron." Judges 16:1-3

Samson was at war with the Philistines most of his life. He outwitted them with riddles, set the tails of foxes on fire in their fields, killed hundreds of their men with only the jawbone of a donkey. The Philistines hated Samson on every level and plotted to take his life repeatedly. In the account of Judges 16:1-3, Samson took hold of the doors of the city gate and the two posts, put them on his shoulders, and carried them to the top of the hill in Hebron as a sign of superiority and victory.

We can imagine Samson carrying the wood of the doors, and the two large posts, on his back as he makes his way up the hill. Substantial as he was, he, no doubt, strained under the load, but he intended to show the Philistines a thing or two and to make a demonstration of victory over them.

"And He must win the battle."

Interestingly, Samson's display of victory on the hill in front of Hebron was followed up with a tremendous victory for the entire Israelite camp. Only it was not in a manner that Samson had envisioned or desired. We read the following in the remaining verses of this same chapter:

> *"And the Philistines seized him and gouged out his eyes and brought*
> *him down to Gaza and bound him with bronze shackles. And he*
> *ground at the mill in the prison.[22] But the hair of his head began to*
> *grow again after it had been shaved.[23] Now the lords of the Philistines*
> *gathered to offer a great sacrifice to Dagon their god and to rejoice,*
> *and they said, "Our god has given Samson our enemy into our*
> *hand."[24] And when the people saw him, they praised their god. For*
> *they said, "Our god has given our enemy into our hand, the ravager*
> *of our country, who has killed many of us."[25] And when their hearts*
> *were merry, they said, "Call Samson, that he may entertain us."*
> *So they called Samson out of the prison, and he entertained them.*
> *They made him stand between the pillars. 26And Samson said to*
> *the young man who held him by the hand, "Let me feel the pillars*
> *on which the house rests, that I may lean against them."[27] Now the*
> *house was full of men and women. All the lords of the Philistines*

were there, and on the roof there were about 3,000 men and women, who looked on while Samson entertained.[28] Then Samson called to the LORD and said, "O Lord GOD, please remember me and please strengthen me only this once, O God, that I may be avenged on the Philistines for my two eyes."[29] And Samson grasped the two middle pillars on which the house rested, and he leaned his weight against them, his right hand on the one and his left hand on the other.[30] And Samson said, "Let me die with the Philistines." Then he bowed with all his strength, and the house fell upon the lords and upon all the people who were in it. So the dead whom he killed at his death were more than those whom he had killed during his life." Judges 16:21-30

Question 2. What was the physical positioning of Samson's body when he died?

Question 3. According to the record of Samson's death in verse 30, what did the death of Samson accomplish?

Samson went from carrying the wood on his back to the top of the hill in victory to his death because Delilah seduced him into revealing the secret of his strength, which allowed the Philistines to capture him, gouge out his eyes, and set him to grinding a mill. We know the story; it is one of the best-known stories of the Bible, inspiring movies and songs down through the years.

It is an incredible life story! The Lord's chosen, Samson, carried the wood up the hill in a demonstration of victory over his enemies, followed shortly by the death of Samson through which he truly did defeat his enemies. Some ancient writers, commenting on this story of Samson's death, tell us how the victory Samson won at his death delivered the Israelites from the rule of the Philistines.

"And He must win the battle."

The picture of the house falling on those evil Philistines is an illustration of Ecclesiastes 9:12:

> *"For man does not know his time. Like fish that are taken in an evil net, and like birds that are caught in a snare, so the children of man are snared at an evil time, when it suddenly falls upon them." Ecclesiastes 9:12*

And the picture of Samson defeating the enemy through his death points us to Hebrews 2:14-15:

> *"Since therefore the children share in flesh and blood, he himself likewise partook of the same things, that through death he might destroy the one who has the power of death, that is, the devil, [15] and deliver all those who through fear of death were subject to lifelong slavery." Hebrews 2:14-15*

> **Question 4.** According to Hebrews 2:14, what did Jesus accomplish through His death?
>
> _____
>
> _____
>
> _____
>
> _____

Question 5. According to Hebrews 2:15, what did Jesus accomplish through His death?

_____

_____

_____

_____

The death of Jesus Christ accomplished numerous things, as we have been studying all through these lessons. Two of these accomplishments were the destruction of the devil and the release of Satan's captives, as stated in Hebrews 2:14-15. These two things are pictured for us in the story of Samson; through Samson's death, he destroyed the enemy and released the Israelites from the tyranny of the Philistines. Through his death, He put the enemy to open shame and triumphed over them, pointing forward to the work that Jesus would do for us.

> "And having disarmed the powers and authorities, he made a public spectacle of them, triumphing over them by the cross."
> Colossians 2:15 (NIV)

> "And He must win the battle."

And Jesus did win the battle for us through His death. He triumphed over the enemy, put them to open shame, released captives, and brought victory to every child of God throughout the ages.

Question 6. Do you understand that by yourself you cannot win the battle over temptation, sin, the flesh, or the devil, but that Jesus Christ won the battle for you through the cross? Can you recall a time of striving in your own strength and losing, and then finding victory through Jesus Christ? Please share:

_____

_____

_____

_____

Layla writes, *"Yes! For years I've attempted to "rebuild" myself emotionally. I've tried self-help books, a counselor, looking to the world for role models, and nothing seemed to fill the enormous void that prevented me from experiencing real joy. When I finally stopped running and pledged my life to God in June 2002, everything changed for the better. Jesus has completely transformed me. He has removed doubt, fear, and self-confidence to fill me with his love and given me confidence in Him that is growing every day. There is no way I could have ever left my misery behind apart from Christ."*

Kathy writes, *"Without God, Himself, intervening in my life, I would have continued in horrible bondage, a slave to food and laziness. I was defeated and lapping up any new diet, any new "answer" the world offered. Then, in God's mercy, He brought me to Setting Captives Free, and I learned that Jesus not only saved me from the penalty of sin but also the power of sin in my life. I was helpless without His intervention. I have been set free by Christ Himself. I am no longer a glutton. He is also saving me from other areas of bondage in my life as well. He is making it real to me that when I am weak, then He is strong. His grace is sufficient for me."*

Victory through Faith
in the Cross

$\mathcal{I}$n recent lessons, we have been studying how the cross of Jesus Christ provides us with victory over sin. Experiencing the freedom Jesus gives us from habitual sin should rejoice our hearts! Most of us previously tried long and hard to break free on our own, only to discover that we were genuinely captive to the power of temptation and sin; but now, like King David in the following verses, we rejoice in God's victory on our behalf:

> *"O LORD, in your strength the king rejoices, and in your victory how greatly he exults! His glory is great through your victory; splendor and majesty you bestow on him." Psalm 21:1,5*

One of the most significant truths about our victory over sin is that real victory and our faith are inextricably linked:

> *"For everyone who has been born of God overcomes the world. And this is the victory that has overcome the world—our faith.[5] Who is it that overcomes the world except the one who believes that Jesus is the Son of God?" 1 John 5:4-5*

Question 1. According to 1 John 5:4, what happens when one becomes *"born of God"*?

Question 2. According to 1 John 5:4, what is it that enables us to overcome the world?

_____

_____

_____

_____

Question 3. According to 1 John 5:5, what is the object of this world-conquering faith?

_____

_____

_____

_____

Incredibly, simple belief in Jesus Christ enables us to wage war with the devil and win, to conquer our stubborn and weak flesh, and to overcome the allurement and sparkling appeal of the world.

But saving faith is not necessarily simplistic faith. In other words, faith that saves and enables us to overcome the world is not simply "believing in Jesus." The word "faith" in 1 John 4:4 does not mean mere "belief," for the demons believe in Christ (James 2:19). Instead, "our faith" is a trusting of our entire life, our soul, our destiny and eternity, to the Person and work of Jesus Christ. Faith that overcomes is believing, in our hearts, that God accepted the payment of Jesus Christ on our behalf, that we are saved from God's wrath through Jesus, and that God raised Christ from the dead for our justification. Victorious faith believes that since Jesus died, we are forgiven, and since He has risen, we are accepted.

So, where do we get this biblical faith that overcomes? In the passages of Scripture that follow, we see that faith is a gift from God, and it comes through hearing and ingesting God's Word.

"looking to Jesus, the founder and perfecter of our faith, who for the joy that was set before him endured the cross, despising the shame, and is seated at the right hand of the throne of God." Hebrews 12:2

"For by the grace given to me I say to everyone among you not to think of himself more highly than he ought to think, but to think with sober judgment, each according to the measure of faith that God has assigned." Romans 12:3

"For by grace you have been saved through faith. And this is not your own doing; it is the gift of God," Ephesians 2:8

"So faith comes from hearing, and hearing through the word of Christ." Romans 10:17

In the famous Old Testament story of David and Goliath, there is a beautiful picture of both the cross of Jesus Christ and the victory that comes through faith in Him. Look with me:

"And David said to Saul, "Let no man's heart fail because of him. Your servant will go and fight with this Philistine."³³ And Saul said to David, "You are not able to go against this Philistine to fight with him, for you are but a youth, and he has been a man of war from his youth."³⁴ But David said to Saul, "Your servant used to keep sheep for his father. And when there came a lion, or a bear, and took a lamb from the flock,³⁵ I went after him and struck him and delivered it out of his mouth. And if he arose against me, I caught him by his beard and struck him and killed him.³⁶ Your servant has struck down both lions and bears, and this uncircumcised Philistine shall be like one of them, for he has defied the armies of the living God."³⁷ And David said, "The

LORD who delivered me from the paw of the lion and from the paw of the bear will deliver me from the hand of this Philistine." And Saul said to David, "Go, and the LORD be with you!" 1 Samuel 17:32-37

Question 4. In the exchange between David and Saul, in what way do we see David's strong faith in God?

_____

_____

_____

_____

Saul's statements to David were logical and reasonable, but they were dead wrong. He said to David, *"you are not able to go against this Philistine to fight with him, for you are but a youth and he has been a man of war from his youth."* Saul's statement entirely left out God, and though what he said was well-reasoned and plausible, it was wrong because he gave no consideration whatsoever to God.

David's faith in God is seen as he recalls the victories God had given him over *"the paw of the lion"* and *"the paw of the bear."* In other words, David was, in essence, saying, "God was *there then*, He will be *here now*." David's faith was not in his ability, but rather in God's ability to bring victory for His people. Simply put, David believed God would help him in his desire to honor God.

Now, let's look for the glorious picture of the cross of Jesus Christ in this same story:

> *"Then David said to the Philistine, "You come to me with a sword and with a spear and with a javelin, but I come to you in the name of the LORD of hosts, the God of the armies of Israel, whom you have defied. This day the LORD will deliver you into my hand, and I will strike you down and cut off your head. And I will give the dead bodies of the host of the Philistines this*

day to the birds of the air and to the wild beasts of the earth, that all the earth may know that there is a God in Israel, and that all this assembly may know that the LORD saves not with sword and spear. For the battle is the LORD's, and he will give you into our hand." When the Philistine arose and came and drew near to meet David, David ran quickly toward the battle line to meet the Philistine. And David put his hand in his bag and took out a stone and slung it and struck the Philistine on his forehead. The stone sank into his forehead, and he fell on his face to the ground. So, David prevailed over the Philistine with a sling and with a stone, and struck the Philistine and killed him. There was no sword in the hand of David. Then David ran and stood over the Philistine and took his sword and drew it out of its sheath and killed him and cut off his head with it. When the Philistines saw that their champion was dead, they fled." 1 Samuel 17:45-51

Question 5. What comparison is made in 1 Samuel 17:45?

_____

_____

_____

_____

Question 6. What general truth is taught in 1 Samuel 17:45?

_____

_____

_____

_____

Question 7. According to 1 Samuel 17:51, what did David use to kill Goliath?

_____

_____

_____

_____

Question 8. According to 1 Samuel 17:51, what was the outcome of the battle?

_____

_____

_____

_____

1 Samuel 17:45-51 contains life-changing truth for us. David's battle is much like our own: the devil is a giant who is much stronger than we are, much smarter than we are; he has been honing his skills against believers for ages. We would have no hope of winning a battle against him on our own.

But the "Son of David" (Matthew 22:42) came to fight the enemy in our place because He was concerned with the honor of God's Name. Jesus fought the "giant" Satan for us! He took death, the devil's own weapon, and used it to destroy the devil and bring victory to all believers.

Consider: *"Since therefore the children share in flesh and blood, he himself likewise partook of the same things, that through death he might destroy the one who has the power of death, that is, the devil," Hebrews 2:14*

Question 9. How does Hebrews 2:14 compare with 1 Samuel 17:51?

_____

_____

_____

_____

Yes, Jesus Christ took death, Satan's own weapon, and destroyed the devil with it. Jesus' death brought victory to all of God's people, just as David's triumph over Goliath brought victory to the whole Israelite nation. Hallelujah!

Today's lesson was about faith that brings victory. David's faith enabled him to overcome the world, the flesh, and the devil of a giant. Our faith in the gospel enables us to overcome the world, the flesh, and the giant of a devil. But our victory, like David's, is really Jesus' victory that He won at the cross. As the verses, we opened this lesson with, say:

> *"O LORD, in your strength the king rejoices, and in your victory how greatly he exults! His glory is great through your victory; splendor and majesty you bestow on him." Psalm 21:1,5*

Just as the old hymn says, *"Faith is the victory, we know, that overcomes the world.*[35]

---

35   https://hymnary.org/text/encamped_along_the_hills_of_light

The Cross Provides Healing
for the Soul

*A*s I write, I am overlooking the Pacific Ocean on the Oregon Coast, where my family is staying for a few days. The windows are open, and I can see the beautiful white waves billowing up and hear them crashing down on the rocks below. The smell of the ocean air is so fresh and invigorating, and I love to watch the seagulls dive and swoop over the sandy beach and then fly away with their favorite catch. It is a beautiful view here in this place accompanied by all the ocean sounds and smells. It is such a delight; some might call it cathartic!

But is it *really* cathartic (i.e., therapeutic, refreshing, healing, liberating)? Many people use the word "cathartic" for a temporal experience, such as our current stay at the beach; by that, they usually mean that the experience has been both calming to their nerves and healing for their souls. Well, as much as I enjoy it here in this calm and peaceful setting, and while I agree that it is indeed calming to the nerves, I would have to say that no external environment is ever *truly* healing for the soul. If it were, everyone who lives here in the Northwest on or near the ocean would have no unrest in their souls, no troubling conscience, no fear of God's wrath, and no sense of impurity in their souls. On the other hand, those who live in other parts of the world where there is no ocean would be defiled, agitated, and all at unrest.

The soul-stirring hymn, "*It is Well with My Soul*" was written by a brokenhearted Horatio Spafford as he was sailing to Europe to meet up with his grieving wife, who had survived the shipwreck they took the life of their daughters. As his ship sailed near the place where his daughters were lost at sea, he wrote these words:

When peace, like a river, attendeth my way,
When sorrows like sea billows roll;
Whatever my lot, Thou has taught me to say,
It is well; it is well, with my soul.[36]
But why was there peace attending Horatio's way? Why was it
well with his soul? Another verse provides us the answer:
My sin, oh, the bliss of this glorious thought!
My sin, not in part but the whole,
Is nailed to the cross, and I bear it no more,
Praise the Lord, praise the Lord, O my soul![37]

It was well with his soul, and it is well with mine, because of the cross! When we grasp the fact that our sin, *"not in part but the whole, is nailed to the cross,"* we are both healed and liberated in our souls. When we understand that we bear our sin no more because Jesus took it all on the cross. At the cross of Christ, we are restored to wholeness, comforted in our sorrows, and set free from sin!

No, it is not an environment that brings true healing and liberation to the soul. At the moment, I have a beautiful view and sights, sounds, and smells I am enjoying, but it is not truly cathartic.

True healing for the soul comes directly from the cross of Jesus Christ. The cross is truly the "tree of life," for, in it, we see Jesus dying our death and providing us life. At this tree of life, there is a great exchange that happens as Jesus takes my wretchedness and provides me with His righteousness.

In the book of Revelation, a description of heaven is provided in great detail. Part of that description is about the tree of life, its location, and its function:

> *"Then the angel showed me the river of the water of life, bright as crystal, flowing from the throne of God and of the Lamb[2] through the middle of the street of the city; also, on either side of the river, the tree of life with its twelve kinds of fruit, yielding its fruit each month. The leaves of the tree were for the healing of the nations.[3]*

36   https://hymnary.org/text/when_peace_like_a_river_attendeth_my_way

37   https://hymnary.org/text/when_peace_like_a_river_attendeth_my_way

No longer will there be anything accursed, but the throne of God and of the Lamb will be in it, and his servants will worship him."
Revelation 22:1-3

Question 1. Where was the tree of life located?

_____

_____

_____

_____

Question 2. What is the purpose of this tree?

_____

_____

_____

_____

Question 3. How does this tree of life compare with and illustrate the function of the cross?

_____

_____

_____

_____

It is appropriate to see the tree of life as a picture of the cross of Jesus Christ because both give life and are for the healing of the nations. Multitudes of those dead in sins and trespasses have been born again at the cross of Jesus Christ. Millions of sin-sick souls, under the burden of guilt and languishing in sin, have found true healing for their souls at the foot of the cross.

One of the clearest presentations of the gospel of Jesus Christ is in the Old Testament book of Isaiah, chapter 53. Isaiah describes the cross as God laying on Jesus *"the iniquity of us all"* (verse 6) and Jesus as the lamb led to the slaughter cut off from the land of the living *"for the transgression of my people"* (verse 8). And in the middle of this vivid description of the death of Jesus Christ, this is said about the effects of His death:

> *"But he was wounded for our transgressions; he was crushed for our iniquities; upon him was the chastisement that brought us peace, and with his stripes we are healed." Isaiah 53:5*

Question 4. According to Isaiah 53:5, what brings us peace?

_____

_____

_____

_____

Question 5. According to Isaiah 53:5, with what are we healed?

_____

_____

_____

_____

In context, Isaiah 53:5 is referring to spiritual healing, healing from sin, and 1 Peter 2:24 clarifies and reiterates that spiritual healing is the purpose of the cross:

> *"He himself bore our sins in his body on the tree, that we might die to sin and live to righteousness. By his wounds you have been healed." 1 Peter 2:24*

Question 6. According to 1 Peter 2:24, why did Jesus bear our sins in His own body on the tree?

_____

_____

_____

_____

Question 7. According to 1 Peter 2:24, of what have we been healed?

_____

_____

_____

_____

To see an illustration of how God does this healing in our lives, read and consider the following verses from Psalm 107. Specifically, take note of how God deals with those who are distressed because of their sin:

> "Some wandered in desert wastes, finding no way to a city to dwell in;⁵ hungry and thirsty, their soul fainted within them.⁶ Then they cried to the LORD in their trouble, and he delivered them from their distress.⁷ He led them by a straight way till they reached a city to dwell in.⁸ Let them thank the LORD for his steadfast love, for his wondrous works to the children of men!⁹ For he satisfies the longing soul, and the hungry soul he fills with good things.¹⁰ Some sat in darkness and in the shadow of death, prisoners in affliction and in irons,¹¹ for they had rebelled against the words of God, and spurned the counsel of the Most High.¹² So he bowed their hearts down with hard labor; they fell down, with none to help.¹³ Then they cried to the LORD in their

trouble, and he delivered them from their distress.[14] He brought them out of darkness and the shadow of death, and burst their bonds apart.[15] Let them thank the LORD for his steadfast love, for his wondrous works to the children of men![16] For he shatters the doors of bronze and cuts in two the bars of iron.[17] Some were fools through their sinful ways, and because of their iniquities suffered affliction;[18] they loathed any kind of food, and they drew near to the gates of death.[19] Then they cried to the LORD in their trouble, and he delivered them from their distress.[20] He sent out his word and healed them, and delivered them from their destruction.[21] Let them thank the LORD for his steadfast love, for his wondrous works to the children of men![22] And let them offer sacrifices of thanksgiving, and tell of his deeds in songs of joy![23] Some went down to the sea in ships, doing business on the great waters;[24] they saw the deeds of the LORD, his wondrous works in the deep.[25] For he commanded and raised the stormy wind, which lifted up the waves of the sea.[26] They mounted up to heaven; they went down to the depths; their courage melted away in their evil plight;[27] they reeled and staggered like drunken men and were at their wits' end.[28] Then they cried to the LORD in their trouble, and he delivered them from their distress.[29] He made the storm be still, and the waves of the sea were hushed.[30] Then they were glad that the waters were quiet, and he brought them to their desired haven.[31] Let them thank the LORD for his steadfast love, for his wondrous works to the children of men! [32] Let them extol him in the congregation of the people, and praise him in the assembly of the elders." Psalms 107:4-32

In Psalm 107, we see the history of the nation of Israel presented in four illustrations. In verses 4-9, we see them as *"wilderness wanderers,"* who are lost and can't find their way out of the desert. In verses 10-16, we see them as *"chained captives,"* who are in a dark prison of their own making because they rebelled against the words of God. In verses 17-22, we see them as *"sin-sick souls,"* who are desperately ill, loathing food, and drawing near to the gates of death because of their foolish and sinful ways. In verses 23-32, we see them as *"tempest-tossed travelers"* who are battered by a storm.

In the first illustration, we see God answering the desperate prayer of the wilderness wanderers as He becomes the "Deliverer of all Distresses" and the "Satisfier of the soul" (Psalm 107:6-9). In the second illustration, we see God answering the desperate cry of the chained captive as He becomes the "Bondage Breaker" for those in prison, helping them out of their self-forged jail cell (Psalm 107:14-16). In the fourth illustration, we see God helping the "tempest-tossed travelers" by becoming the "Storm Stiller" for them, bringing them to their desired haven (Psalm 107:29-30).

Notice now that the third illustration presents our God as the "Powerful Physician" to the sin-sick soul. Verse 20 tells us, *"He sent forth His Word and healed them."* Oh yes, there is true healing for sin-sickness in God's Word.

Two thousand years ago, God sent forth His Word of healing. His Word became flesh and dwelt among us in the Person of Jesus Christ (John 1:14). He grew up sinless and perfect, helping all around Him, and doing good. He healed the sick, raised the dead, cured the leper, fed the poor, and did so many other good things that if they were all to be written, even the whole earth could not contain them (John 21:25). In return, He was falsely accused by His own people, mocked, judged wrongly, and condemned to death. Before His crucifixion, He was beaten, scourged, tormented, and tortured. Then He was hung between two criminals on a cruel Roman cross. Why? Why did all this happen to Him? Why did He willingly lay down His life?

> *"He sent out his word and healed them and delivered them from their destruction." Psalm 107:20*

Ah, here is the healing power of the cross! God sent out His Word, Jesus Christ, Who died on the cross to heal us, dear friend, from our sin-sickness and to deliver us from our self-destructive ways.

As I sit here looking out over the beauty of the ocean, seeing the white foam of the waves, hearing the call of the seagulls, and smelling the fresh ocean air, I am thankful that our God has made an environment like this for our delight. But as I have written this lesson, I have been crying tears of brokenhearted joy. I have seen once again the immensity of the sacrifice of Jesus Christ on my behalf. I have been delighting in the forgiveness and new life I have found at the cross. It is not the ocean, the fresh air, and the seagulls that bring healing to my soul. It is the cross!

It is hard to imagine the immensity of the pain that Jesus underwent at the cross. He was beaten, whipped, crushed, bruised, scourged, and tortured. He was trampled, battered, cursed, mocked, spit upon, struck, and marred beyond human recognition (Isaiah 52:14). It is even more amazing to grasp the truth that all this suffering was for our healing. He was "chastised" to bring us peace, and *"by His stripes, we are healed."*

If you want catharsis, look to the cross of Christ. Jesus purchased it for you there.

Question 8. Please provide any closing thoughts you have on this lesson.

_____

_____

_____

_____

Irene writes, *"Jesus is our strength and righteousness. Help me understand it, Lord, help me take it in, what it meant for you, the Holy One, to remove my sin. Father, I believe, I step out in faith in your work at Calvary, your strength, your healing, your victory."*

Samantha writes, *"For several years I have been admonished by the Lord to linger at Gethsemane and the foot of the cross. I attempted to do this, but this is the first real study that I have found that has given me clarity on why He would have me do this. It is because God loves me and wants me to know the depth of His love for me, what Jesus willingly went through on my behalf. He wants me to know what He did for me. I was sexually abused as a child, and I hid my true self away and withdrew even from God for many years because I did not want to be hurt. I praise God that He would not leave me there but has shown Himself to me. God has healed me of many diseases of the heart, mind, soul, and body. He did this for me on the cross because He loved me. I* *struggle to understand. I, too, am sitting here in tears; it is hard for this finite mind to comprehend. He's breaking the hard shell I built around my heart. I don't have to be afraid anymore; I don't have to hide anymore. Jesus' death bought my freedom; He wants me to live and live a life in, with, and through Him. He was there when I was hurt, He has always been there with me, and He will always be there with me. I can trust Him; I can let Him love me. I am free to live again. Thank You, Father, thank You."*

The Cross Provides Fullness

"For in him the whole fullness of deity dwells bodily,[10] and you have been filled in him, who is the head of all rule and authority." Colossians 2:9-10

The Bible describes unbelievers as being like "chaff" (Psalm 1:4), waves of the sea, full of "foam" (Jude 1:13), and "empty" (1 Peter 1:18). These descriptions form the understanding that the unconverted are empty shells (like chaff), without substance, full of air (like foam), who live meaningless lives (futile ways). This ongoing emptiness is one of the causes of the mass of humanity rushing to forbidden relationships, drugs, alcohol, materialism, pornography, etc. Unbelievers are attempting to fill the void that is so clearly within them. And in their rush to grab all of life they can before it is gone completely, they become filled with *"all manner of unrighteousness, covetousness, malice"* (Romans 1:29).

Believers, on the other hand, have been *"filled in Him"* (Colossians 2:10)! When Jesus Christ came into our lives, He filled our hearts. Indeed, our lives are *"hid with Christ in God"* and *"filled with all the fullness of God"* (Ephesians 3:19).

Our fullness in Christ is a wonderful blessing from God, and, as we have noted many times now, the cross is the grounds or basis for all the blessings we receive in Jesus Christ. Let us now consider some passages of Scripture and their implications for the believer's fullness in Christ:

> *"And they were striking his head with a reed and spitting on him and kneeling down in homage to him.[20] And when they had mocked him, they stripped him of the purple cloak and put his own clothes on him. And they led him out to crucify him.[21] And*

they compelled a passerby, Simon of Cyrene, who was coming in from the country, the father of Alexander and Rufus, to carry his cross.²² And they brought him to the place called Golgotha (which means Place of a Skull). ³ And they offered him wine mixed with myrrh, but he did not take it.²⁴ And they crucified him and divided his garments among them, casting lots for them, to decide what each should take." Mark 15:19-24

Question 1. Please list all the abuses Jesus endured that are mentioned in Mark 15:19-20. The first is: "striking his head..."

_____

_____

_____

_____

Question 2. According to Mark 15:22, where was Jesus Christ crucified?

_____

_____

_____

_____

Question 3. According to Mark 15:22, what is the meaning of the name "Golgotha?"

_____

_____

_____

_____

Mark 15:22 is heart-breaking for sure. Yet we are not to weep for Christ, but rather weep for our sins, and weep in repentance (Luke 23:28). Every statement listed in this passage is full of meaning for the meditative Christian who feeds on *"every word that proceeds from the mouth of God"* (Deuteronomy 8:3). Every word of God is instructive and full of life for those who believe.

In this case, the word *"Golgotha"* is significant. Golgotha means "the place of the skull," and Golgotha's hill does indeed resemble a skull. If you look at a picture of Golgotha, you will see the "nose" and "eye sockets" and "forehead" of "the skull."

Jerusalem is said to be "the city of seven hills," and the Romans crucified criminals at many places in the city, so why did Jesus die on this particular hill? Why did God choose this hill that looks like a skull for His Son's death?

Think for a moment of what a skull is. The Greek word used by Mark is "kranion," pronounced "kran-ee'-on." It is the root word for our English word "cranium." Now we know that a cranium can be on the shoulders of a live man, whereas a "skull" is an *empty head* or a *dead head*.

Please review the following Scriptures, noting what Jesus Christ is called in all of them:

> *"But I want you to understand that the head of every man is Christ, the head of a wife is her husband, and the head of Christ is God."*
> *1 Corinthians 11:3*

> *"And he put all things under his feet and gave him as head over all things to the church,"* *Ephesians 1:22*

> *"Rather, speaking the truth in love, we are to grow up in every way into him who is the head, into Christ,"* *Ephesians 4:15*

> *"For the husband is the head of the wife even as Christ is the head of the church, his body, and is himself its Savior."* *Ephesians 5:23*

> *"And he is the head of the body, the church. He is the beginning, the firstborn from the dead, that in everything he might be preeminent."* *Colossians 1:18*

"...and you have been filled in him, who is the head of all rule and authority." Colossians 2:10

Question 4. What do all these Scriptures call Jesus Christ?
- ☐ The Foundation
- ☐ The Heart
- ☐ The Head

By way of summary, Jesus Christ is *"head of man," "head of the church," "head of the body,"* and *"head of all rule and authority."* Calling Jesus *"the head"* conveys that He is the leader, the director, the principal, the supreme authority, etc.—even as the head directs the body.

And as *"the head,"* Jesus accomplished some significant work for the body. Please read and record what Jesus Christ did in each of the Scriptures listed below:

"...for this is my blood of the covenant, which is poured out for many for the forgiveness of sins." Matthew 26:28

Question 5. According to Matthew 26:28, what did Jesus do?

_____

_____

_____

_____

"Have this mind among yourselves, which is yours in Christ Jesus,⁶ who, though he was in the form of God, did not count equality with God a thing to be grasped,⁷ but made himself nothing, taking the form of a servant, being born in the likeness of men. And being found in human form,⁸ he humbled himself by becoming obedient to the point of death, even death on a cross." Philippians 2:5-8

Question 6. According to Philippians 2:7, what did Jesus Christ do?

_____

_____

_____

_____

"Then Jesus, calling out with a loud voice, said, "Father, into your hands I commit my spirit!" And having said this he breathed his last." Luke 23:46

Question 7. According to Luke 23:46, what did Jesus Christ do?

_____

_____

_____

_____

"For you know the grace of our Lord Jesus Christ, that though he was rich, yet for your sake he became poor, so that you by his poverty might become rich." 2 Corinthians 8:9

Question 8. According to 2 Corinthians 8:9, what did Jesus Christ do?

_____

_____

_____

_____

In these verses, we see that Jesus Christ emptied Himself, pouring out His life's blood for the forgiveness of sins, humbled Himself, making Himself "nothing," for our sakes He became "poor," and then, He gave up His Spirit and died.

The connection has become evident. Jesus Christ, the head of the body, the church, of man," and of all authority, emptied Himself, became nothing, and died on the cross at Golgotha, the "place of the skull." Jesus Christ died at the place of the empty and dead head.

And what was the purpose of His death? Well, among many other things, Jesus emptied Himself that we might receive of His fullness, grace upon grace.

> *"(John bore witness about him, and cried out, "This was he of whom I said, 'He who comes after me ranks before me, because he was before me.' ")[16] And from his fullness we have all received, grace upon grace." John 1:15-16*

Jesus counted equality with God a thing not to be grasped but emptied Himself and became a servant (Philippians 2:6-7), that we of His fullness might receive grace. He came to do God's will (Hebrews 10:5-7).

Think of the implications of this glorious truth. We no longer need to seek fullness by gratifying our flesh, following the devil, or the allurements of this world. No more do people have to live life attempting to get all the life they can before they die, to acquire more and more possessions, to fill their empty hearts with empty things, but instead, those who become believers in Christ have fullness from Christ *in themselves* to give to others.

> *"You make known to me the path of life; in your presence there is fullness of joy; at your right hand are pleasures forevermore." Psalm 16:11*

> *"And he put all things under his feet and gave him as head over all things to the church,[23] which is his body, the fullness of him who fills all in all." Ephesians 1:22-23*

> *"...so that Christ may dwell in your hearts through faith-that you, being rooted and grounded in love,[18] may have strength to*

comprehend with all the saints what is the breadth and length and height and depth,[19] and to know the love of Christ that surpasses knowledge, that you may be filled with all the fullness of God." Ephesians 3:17-19

"And he gave the apostles, the prophets, the evangelists, the pastors and teachers,[12] to equip the saints for the work of ministry, for building up the body of Christ,[13] until we all attain to the unity of the faith and of the knowledge of the Son of God, to mature manhood, to the measure of the stature of the fullness of Christ,[14] so that we may no longer be children, tossed to and fro by the waves and carried about by every wind of doctrine, by human cunning, by craftiness in deceitful schemes." Ephesians 4:11-14

Believers all down through history have found this fullness from God. Examine this fullness for God's people in the following texts.

"Abraham breathed his last and died in a good old age, an old man and full [of years], and was gathered to his people." Genesis 25:8

In the above verse, notice that the words "of years" were added by the translators. Abraham died not empty but full.

David, the shepherd boy who became king, sang, "You prepare a table before me in the presence of my enemies; you anoint my head with oil; my cup overflows." Psalm 23:5

So, Abraham died *"old and full,"* and David's cup *"overflowed"* for this has been the condition of all believers down through every age, all in anticipation of Him Who would come, empty Himself and die, at Golgotha, that we might live and be full.

Question 9. What are your final thoughts on this lesson?

_____

_____

_____

_____

Isabel writes, *"What love was this! He gave His all, holding nothing back, He became poor that I might be rich. He became sin that I might be righteous. The Holy Mighty Eternal God loved me so much; I can thank Him by presenting my body a living sacrifice in worship and love."*

Ricky writes, *"He emptied Himself and made Himself nothing— what physical and spiritual connotations. The only Being ever to be completely man and completely God, Who was full of the knowledge and wisdom of the entire universe, allowed His blood to be drained and His throne to be empty so that we could be filled with His Spirit. I apprehend it, but will never, ever comprehend it. Thank you, my beautiful Savior!"*

Final Words from the Cross

A person's final words in this life are usually significant to their loved ones. Through the ages, friends, and family members have leaned in to hear and understand the last words uttered by their friend, parent, spouse, or child before they die. Dying words are often cherished, repeated, and sometimes they are life changing. So, it is for us who believe in Jesus.

In the lessons to come, we will be remembering and studying all that Jesus said while He was hanging on the cross. These words are a precious treasure for us to mine. Consider them with me now:

1. *"And Jesus said, "Father, forgive them, for they know not what they do." Luke 23:34*

2. *"And he said to him, "Truly, I say to you, today you will be with me in Paradise." Luke 23:43*

3. *"When Jesus saw his mother and the disciple whom he loved standing nearby, he said to his mother, "Woman, behold, your son!"[27] Then he said to the disciple, "Behold, your mother!" And from that hour the disciple took her to his own home." John 19:26-27*

4. *"And about the ninth hour Jesus cried out with a loud voice, saying, "Eli, Eli, lema sabachthani?" that is, "My God, my God, why have you forsaken me?" Matthew 27:46*

5. "After this, Jesus, knowing that all was now finished, said (to fulfill the Scripture), "I thirst." John 19:28

6. "When Jesus had received the sour wine, he said, "It is finished," and he bowed his head and gave up his spirit." John 19:30

7. "Then Jesus, calling out with a loud voice, said, "Father, into your hands I commit my spirit!" And having said this he breathed his last." Luke 23:46

In the next seven lessons, we will study through each of these sentences to understand their significance and see more clearly the glory, suffering, love, and salvation of Jesus.

Let's begin:

"And Jesus said, "Father, forgive them, for they know not what they do." Luke 23:34

Question 1. According to Luke 23:34, what did Jesus pray for God to do to His enemies?

_____

_____

_____

_____

Forgiveness! Was there ever a more beautiful word? We all want it, but sometimes we find it hard to give. And yet, Jesus, nailed to a cross, struggling for every breath, prayed aloud for His Father to forgive His enemies. Understanding that Jesus could have put an end to His tormentors at any moment, makes His gracious and costly intercession all the more powerful.

By way of contrast, in Judges 16, we read the final words of Samson:

"Then Samson called to the Lord, saying, "O Lord God, remember me, I pray! Strengthen me; I pray, just this once, O God, that I may with one blow take vengeance on the Philistines for my two eyes!"

Samson's final words were ones of vengeance, and his victory over the Philistines, while significant, was temporary. But Jesus died with love and forgiveness on His lips, and His victory over sin, death, and hell were permanent! What a Savior!

Jesus' prayer for His enemies was not only supernatural, it was also a fulfillment of a prophecy given in Isaiah 53:

"Therefore I will divide him a portion with the many, and he shall divide the spoil with the strong, because he poured out his soul to death and was numbered with the transgressors; yet he bore the sin of many, and made intercession for the transgressors."
Isaiah 53:12

Question 2. How does the last phrase of Isaiah 53:12 compare with Luke 23:34?

_____

_____

_____

_____

Isaiah 53 teaches us that Jesus would:

- be wounded for our transgressions
- be bruised for our iniquities
- carry our sorrows
- be led quietly to death as a lamb led to the slaughter
- pour out His soul unto death while bearing the sins of many
- make intercession for the transgressors.

The context of Isaiah 53 tells us that Isaiah 53:12 is not referring to Jesus' present ministry in Heaven where He *"ever lives to intercede for us"* (Hebrews 7:25), but to the time of His death and His prayer for those who crucified Him. Jesus pleaded for His crucifiers and interceded for His assassins. What shocking grace!

So, the prophecy was for Jesus to *"make intercession for the transgressors,"* and on the cross, Jesus fulfilled it, *"Father, forgive them, for they know not what they do."*

Next, we see that Jesus' prayer of forgiveness gives us an unforgettable example of what He taught in life regarding the godly response of a believer to their enemies. In the Sermon on the Mount, Jesus taught His disciples, *"But I say to you who listen: Love your enemies, do good to those who hate you, bless those who curse you, pray for those who mistreat you."*

Question 3. According to Luke 6:27-28, please list the four actions which Christians are to take when they are wronged.

_____

_____

_____

_____

Question 4. How did Jesus love His enemies, do good to those who hated Him, bless those who cursed Him, and pray for those who mistreated Him as He died on the cross?

_____

_____

_____

_____

Jesus practiced what He preached. On the cross, Jesus loved His enemies, sacrificing Himself for those who cursed Him, doing good to and blessing those who hated Him while praying for those who despitefully used and persecuted Him. Our Lord loved perfectly, as Love *"suffers long and is kind...bears all things...endures all things"* (1 Corinthians 13).

The fact that Jesus' first words from the cross were about forgiveness is so fitting because our forgiveness is what He was securing for us through His death on the cross.

Down through time, doctors have prioritized various things as essential to life—food, clothing, shelter, etc., but such things are temporary. Our primary and eternal need is God's forgiveness because we have all sinned against God and one another.

The world has no real answers as to why people do wrong things. If we were to ask a prison psychiatrist about why this man is a rapist or that woman is a killer, they would not have a precise answer. They might say that heredity and environment play a part, but since these factors are not universal or consistent, the world really does not know why people are the way they are. But God knows because He made us. After Adam sinned, all people were born sinners (Romans 3:23). We cannot fix ourselves (Jeremiah 13:23). So, before the foundations of the world were even laid, God made a way to save us by sending Jesus to die on the cross to secure forgiveness for us.

In ministering to those in habitual sin, my wife and I have discovered that there is a widespread worldly methodology, which teaches the "step method" of how to stop habitual sin or become "sober." Many churches have adopted this method, yet such programs are not sufficient or lasting. Steps toward recovery do not affect a permanent change in a person's nature because they do not deal first and foremost with sin, inherent guilt, or man's need for forgiveness. They leave the person with guilt on their soul, and guilt is like an undertow that drags people back into the ocean of sin. No wonder their catchphrase is "once an addict, always an addict," for their teaching misses the primary and essential truth that sets captives free. On the cross, Jesus begins where these step programs don't even go, with forgiveness of sin and the removal of guilt.

Even those who sin in ignorance are culpable, guilty of their sins, and in need of forgiveness. Ignorance is no excuse, and sins committed in ignorance still need forgiveness. We can see this truth taught in the Old Testament:

"But if you sin unintentionally, and do not observe all these commandments that the LORD has spoken to Moses,²³ all that the LORD has commanded you by Moses, from the day that the LORD gave commandment, and onward throughout your generations,²⁴ then if it was done unintentionally without the knowledge of the congregation, all the congregation shall offer one bull from the herd for a burnt offering, a pleasing aroma to the LORD, with its grain offering and its drink offering, according to the rule, and one male goat for a sin offering.²⁵ And the priest shall make atonement for all the congregation of the people of Israel, and they shall be forgiven, because it was a mistake, and they have brought their offering, a food offering to the LORD, and their sin offering before the LORD for their mistake." Numbers 15:22-25

Question 5. Please list the words from Numbers 15:22-25 which speak of sinning in ignorance.

_____

_____

_____

_____

Question 6. According to Numbers 15:25, what did the priest have to do for the people who sinned unintentionally or by mistake?

_____

_____

_____

All of us have committed sins in ignorance as well as intentional sins, but the good news is that Jesus' sacrifice is sufficient to purchase forgiveness for all sins.

As we close out our lesson, let's see how God answered Jesus' prayer for forgiveness:

> *"And now, brothers, I know that you acted in ignorance, as did also your rulers. But what God foretold by the mouth of all the prophets, that his Christ would suffer, he thus fulfilled. Acts 3:17-18*

> *"And Jesus said, "Father, forgive them, for they know not what they do." Luke 23:34*

Question 7. How does Acts 3:17 compare with Luke 23:34?

_____

_____

_____

_____

Peter was preaching to a large gathering of Jews, and the result of his sermon was that five thousand people were saved from their sins and converted to Christ. Five thousand people received the forgiveness that Jesus prayed for them to have. Peter's phrase, *"you acted in ignorance,"* compares with Jesus' prayer to forgive those who *"know not what they do."*

Jesus was able to not only pray for the forgiveness of those who crucified Him but also to secure their forgiveness through His death in their place. Because of the blood He was shedding, He could pray, *"Father, forgive them."*

My friend, if you are an unbeliever, please hear this good word for you: Jesus Christ prayed for the forgiveness of His crucifiers before they knew of their need for it. Come today and ask Jesus to forgive you; you will discover, no matter how deep your sins, that *"...in Him, we have redemption through His blood, the forgiveness of sins"* (Colossians 1:14) and *"through this One, the forgiveness of sins is announced to you"* (Acts 13:38).

If you are a believer, Jesus' prayer of forgiveness tells you not to fear when the accuser, Satan, comes with reminders of your sins to make you doubt, question, and wonder about your acceptance with God. Jesus *"made atonement for iniquity"* (Daniel 9:24), and therefore no one can *"bring a charge against God's elect"* (Romans 8:33). Without the shedding of blood, there is no forgiveness of sins, but Jesus did shed His blood, and we are forgiven! Rejoice, believer, for your forgiveness was purchased by Christ, your sins were atoned for at the cross, your guilt is removed, and your eternal life is secure!

> *"But with you there is forgiveness, that you may be feared."* Psalm 130:4

> *"Blessed are those whose lawless deeds are forgiven, and whose sins are covered;"* Romans 4:7

> *"Be kind to one another, tenderhearted, forgiving one another, as God in Christ forgave you."* Ephesians 4:32

> *"And you, who were dead in your trespasses and the uncircumcision of your flesh, God made alive together with him, having forgiven us all our trespasses,"* Colossians 2:13

> *"I am writing to you, little children, because your sins are forgiven for his name's sake."* 1 John 2:12

Question 8. What are your thoughts on today's lesson? Please share:

_____

_____

_____

_____

Damian writes, *"This teaching really opened up my understanding. I knew Jesus died for our iniquity, but I never knew how it was* *accomplished. I knew it was by the blood, yes, but the tenets to how and why I never saw before. I have found a new respect for Jesus. He is becoming more of my friend and Savior from this teaching. Just going with the flow, as I have for so many years, was a travesty, and I now see why my witness was such a weak one, for I never had a grasp of what was accomplished for me on the cross. If I did at one time, it surely got muddled over time and the rigors of sustaining the posture of looking the part and not ever having a revelation of what Christ has done for me."*

Rachelle writes, *"I want you guys to know that this study has changed how I view the entire Bible. I was raised by godly parents, who taught me a lot about the Bible. I thought I was pretty knowledgeable, but this study has been opening my eyes to parallels and "types" that I've never seen before. Now when I read His Word, I look for the pictures/types that bring me a deeper knowledge of my Lord. I see things I've never seen before, and I'm getting to know my Jesus on a deeper level. Thank you."*

Words of Life and Hope
from the Cross

*I*n our previous lesson, we began our study of Jesus' final words spoken from His cross before He died. These are precious sentences that our Lord uttered in His last moments while dying to atone for our sins, so we want to lean in, listen, and learn from what Jesus said in His darkest hour. We first heard and understood the importance of Jesus' prayer for the forgiveness of His enemies, and, now, in this lesson, we will take note of how Jesus spoke words of life and hope to the repentant thief on the cross who was hanging next to Him.

> *"There was also an inscription over him, "This is the King of the Jews." One of the criminals who were hanged railed at him, saying, "Are you not the Christ? Save yourself and us!" But the other rebuked him, saying, "Do you not fear God, since you are under the same sentence of condemnation? And we indeed justly, for we are receiving the due reward of our deeds; but this man has done nothing wrong." And he said, "Jesus, remember me when you come into your kingdom." And he said to him, "Truly, I say to you, today you will be with me in paradise." Luke 23:38-43*

Initially, both robbers crucified on either side of Jesus joined the crowd of onlookers in their mockery and ridicule of Jesus (Matthew 27:44). But at some point, one of the thieves came to his senses, turned from his sin, and found pardon through Jesus Christ (Luke 23:40-43). It is this repentant thief and Jesus' words spoken to him that we will consider today.

The pardoned thief represents all who receive the gift of repentance, put faith in Jesus, and experience salvation from their sins; he is a picture of you and me. So, as you think of this thief today, see yourself in his place.

When the Holy Spirit begins to operate on our hearts, He gives us a proper view of ourselves and an accurate understanding of Christ. Let's notice several things this thief came to believe about himself and Jesus.

In Luke 23:38-43, we first notice that the Holy Spirit brought conviction of sin to the heart of this robber.

> **Question 1.** According to Luke 23:38-43, what statements did the thief make that evidence his conviction of sin?
>
> _____
>
> _____
>
> _____
>
> _____

The repentant thief acknowledged his sin and guilt and believed that he was worthy of the sentence of death he had received. He confessed that his punishment was "just" and right. He said to his counterpart, *"We are receiving the due reward of our deeds."* In other words, "I am owed this punishment; I earned my death sentence." He acknowledged his wrong, did not make any excuses for his sins, and did not attempt to shift the blame to others, which is atypical for criminals. Here is a man who sees himself correctly now.

Until the Holy Spirit shows a person the sinfulness of their sin, they will minimize, justify, make excuses, or shift blame to someone else, but once He opens a heart, it cannot unsee its desperate need for salvation through Jesus.

A heart opened by the Holy Spirit admits defeat; it accepts its desperate need for a Savior, which we see in this thief. The repentant thief has no hope of salvation by his own merits, so he looks to Jesus.

> **Question 2.** In Luke 23:42, what request does the robber make to indicate he is at the end of himself?
>
> _____

The converted robber, having seen his situation in the light of truth, in desperation, calls out to Jesus, asking, "*Jesus, remember me when you come into your kingdom.*" This man had no hope in himself or any other, only Jesus.

Likewise, all believers come to know their desperate need for a Savior, but it may not come upon us as quickly as it did with this thief. There is so much pride in the human heart, so much desire to work our way into God's favor that it can take time for us to see that we are "*without strength*" (Romans 5:6), "*impotent*" (John 5:3), and that it is *not by works of righteousness which we do, but by His mercy, He saves us* (Titus 3:5).

By way of example, the prodigal son left his father's house and squandered away all his resources through wild living and began to be in need. But what did he do, where did he go when he first sensed his need? Did he go back to his father, there to plead for mercy? No, he went to *work*. "*Then he went to work for one of the citizens of that country, who sent him into his fields to feed pigs*" (Luke 15:15). He sought to redeem himself, to work his way out of his problems. How like so many today who, when they become aware of their sins, begin to do good works or become religious, attempting to redeem themselves. It took further dawning realizations of his need for the prodigal to understand the severity of his situation, and then to return to his father to plead for mercy. And frequently, it is not until we come to *the end* of our resources that we seek Jesus (Mark 5:26)—just like this thief on the cross.

So, now, we see the thief in his right mind, admitting his wrong, and the rightness of his punishment, and then we see him turning to Jesus for help.

Maybe you do not identify with this thief. Perhaps you acknowledge that you are not all you could be, but you don't see yourself as deserving of death and hell, but what you think does not change the facts. The Bible says that "the carnal mind is *enmity against God:* for it is not subject to the law of God, neither can it be" (Romans 8:7). And "*there is no difference:* for all have sinned and come short of the glory of God" (Romans 3:22-23).

Question 3. Have you recognized that you are lost and hopeless to change on your own? Do you see your need for Jesus to save and sanctify you? Please share.

_____

_____

_____

_____

Earlier, we said that when the Holy Spirit works in our hearts, we come to a correct understanding of not only ourselves as sinners but also of Christ as Savior. Now let's take note of what this changed thief believed about Jesus.

First, he believed that Jesus was *sinless.*

Question 4. According to Luke 23:38-43, what did the thief say that evidenced his understanding of Jesus' sinlessness?

_____

_____

_____

_____

The thief confessed that Jesus "had done *nothing wrong.*" In this way, he added his voice to the numerous others who testified to Jesus' righteousness. Judas said, "I have betrayed *innocent* blood." Pilate testified, "I find *no fault* in Him." Pilate's wife said, "Have nothing to do with this *just* man." And now, as he hangs on the cross, God opens the eyes of this robber to see the faultlessness of Jesus and opens his lips to bear testimony to Jesus' sinlessness.

The repentant robber not only understood that Jesus had done no wrong, but he also accepted Him as Savior.

Question 5. What request does the thief make that indicates his acknowledgment of Christ as Savior?

_____

_____

_____

_____

The thief pleaded, *"Jesus, remember me."* These few words encapsulated this man's hope of salvation, pardon, help, protection, and deliverance through Jesus. And how appropriate was it that the thief asked Jesus to remember him, for as an outcast of society, who else would remember him? The angry mob would undoubtedly forget all about him within days, his friends, if he had any, would forget him in time, and his family had probably disowned him because of his crimes. But, by the power of the Holy Spirit, this man knew that He could call out to Jesus and be received and remembered.

Not only did the thief acknowledge Jesus as the sinless Savior, but he also accepted Jesus as King!

Question 6. What did the thief say that evidenced his understanding of Jesus as King?

_____

_____

_____

_____

The thief said, "Jesus, remember me when you come into your *kingdom.*" Here we can see the fullness and confidence of this man's faith in Jesus because, at the time, Jesus did not look like a king. Instead of sitting on a throne, He was hanging on a cross. Instead of wearing a royal diadem, Jesus was wearing a crown of thorns. Instead of being served by subjects, He was enduring the hate and abuse of an angry mob.

Remember the sign that Pilate had placed above the head of Jesus? It said, *"This is the King of the Jews."* Even though the sign was placed there as a mockery, it was the truth, which God spoke into the heart of the thief, who then believed Jesus to be a King and asked, *"Jesus, remember me when you come into your kingdom."*

But this thief not only believed that Jesus to be a sinless Savior and King; he also dared to hope for a future with Jesus as his King. This thief looked beyond the current dark and grim situation to a bright and hopeful future. He looked past the crown of thorns and saw the crown of glory, past Jesus' cross of humiliation and shame to a day when Jesus would ascend his throne and reign in power and glory!

Some believe that facing death brings clarity and deep understanding, but it is evident that God gave spiritual understanding to this thief in his final moments. This former robber saw himself as wretched, vile, and helpless, and Jesus Christ as the sinless Savior and King Who would come into a glorious kingdom. Though this robber's hands and feet were nailed to a cross, his heart and tongue were set free. With his heart, he believed and was justified, and with his mouth, he confessed and was saved (Romans 10:10).

As we close out this lesson, let us rejoice in the beautiful words of acceptance this thief heard from Jesus Christ when he was *"richly provided an entrance into the kingdom of our Lord and Savior, Jesus Christ"* (2 Peter 1:11) because we believers hear them for us as well.

> **Question 7.** Please write out the request of the thief, and the answer from Jesus as given in Luke 23:42-43:
>
> _____
>
> _____
>
> _____
>
> _____

When we compare the request the thief made with the answer Jesus gave him, it is apparent that, in His usual fashion, Jesus gave far more than the thief asked.

The thief asked to be remembered at some *future* point when Jesus came into His kingdom. Jesus answered, *"Today, you will be with me..."* The thief asked merely to be included in Christ's kingdom, Jesus said, "Today you will be *with me* in Paradise." Oh, how Jesus always does *"exceedingly abundantly more than all we ask or think"* (Ephesians 3:20). He doesn't just bring us into His kingdom, He brings us into His presence, into intimacy *with Him*. Upon his cross of death, this thief received a message of life and hope!

Jesus' promise to the dying thief should stir our souls in hope too. One day we, too, will be dying, and on that day, Jesus' promise will ring out loud and clear, *"Today, you will be with me."* And isn't that the desire of all believing hearts, to be with Christ?

Heaven without Christ would not be heaven. The psalmist sang, *"Whom have I in heaven but You, and earth has nothing I desire but You"* (Psalm 73:25). Paul wrote, *"I desire to depart and be with Christ..."* (Philippians 1:23). And our presence with Him is also the prayer and longing of Christ. Jesus prayed:

> *"Father, I desire that they also, whom you have given me, may be with me where I am, to see my glory that you have given me because you loved me before the foundation of the world." John 17:24*

Finally, the salvation of this dying thief is proof that Jesus is willing to save all who come to Him. The theologian Arthur Pink put it this way:

> *"If Christ received this penitent, believing thief, then none need despair of a welcome if they will but come to Christ. If this dying robber was not beyond the reach of Divine mercy then none are who will respond to the invitations of Divine grace. The Son of Man came 'to seek and to save that which was lost' (Luke 19:10), and none can sink lower than that. The Gospel of Christ is the power of God 'to every one that believeth' (Romans 1:16). O limit not the grace of God. A Savior is provided for the very 'chief of sinners" (1 Timothy 1:15), if only he will believe."*[38]

---

38   Arthur Pink, *The Seven Sayings of the Savior on the Cross*, 1984 Baker Books a division of Baker Book House Company P.O. Box 6287, Grand Rapids, MI 49516-6287

Oh, friend, the believer's life is one of acceptance and hope in Jesus. We rejoice in our approval in Christ and do not despair for those we love who have yet to come to Him. Even at the last minute, they might have their hearts opened and receive the good word that they are received and remembered and will be with Jesus.

Question 8. Please share any final comments or questions you might have about the lesson today.

_____

_____

_____

Di writes, *"The Scripture that immediately came to me was Psalm 27:4, "One thing I ask from the Lord, this only do I seek: that I may dwell in the house of the Lord all the days of my life, to gaze on the beauty of the Lord and to seek him in his temple." That is my desire, and that is not only to attend worship in a man-made building, but for all eternity in the mansions in heaven not made by human hands. The Builder is God and the building is Christ, His body, His Church. I am welling up with joy at this very moment. I haven't been so desirous of feeding upon the Word since my conversion many, many years ago. This study has been a real blessing to my life! Thanks to the Lord and his unending mercies!"*

Words of Love and Care
from the Cross

*I*n these final lessons, we are considering the last words of Jesus that He spoke while on the cross. These words are so precious to us who believe because we have been changed forever through the love of Jesus. Our Lord spoke these words while He hung in agony, atoning for our sins. So far, we have considered Jesus' prophecy fulfilling prayer for the forgiveness of His enemies and His message of life and hope to the repentant robber who asked to be remembered. Now, we draw in closer to hear the words of love and care that Jesus spoke to His mother and the significance they hold for us.

> *"When Jesus saw his mother and the disciple whom he loved standing nearby, he said to his mother, "Woman, behold, your son!" Then he said to the disciple, "Behold, your mother!" And from that hour the disciple took her to his own home." John 19:26-27*

Question 1. According to John 19:26-27, what was on Jesus' heart and mind at this time as He hung dying on the cross?

_____

_____

_____

_____

John 19:26-27 could be summed up with the words love and care. Jesus saw His mother and John *"the disciple whom Jesus loved"* (John 20:2) and spoke directly to them in love. And considering that Jesus was nailed to a cross suffering in every way possible, His thoughtfulness is even more profound. Jesus was actively bleeding, hanging by nails, naked, swollen beyond recognition, thorns piercing his scalp, and through all this, He looks and sees His mother and John, and then summons the strength to speak to them. Can you fathom it? In the throes of death, Jesus honors His mother and cares for her perfectly.

Indeed, every fiber of Jesus' being was always concerned for others, not for Himself. Especially in death, His mind and heart were intent on loving and caring for others. Jesus saw His mother—her hurt and pain—and He had compassion for her and arranged for her care through John. This loving act was beautiful, but how much more the eternal act of mercy, love, and care Jesus arranged for all who believe.

From His cross, Jesus saw you and me too, and through His death, He arranged for both our temporary and eternal needs. But His love and attention for us did not stop at the cross; Jesus continues to see us and care for us.

> *"For we do not have a high priest who is unable to sympathize with our weaknesses, but one who in every respect has been tempted as we are, yet without sin.*[16] *Let us then with confidence draw near to the throne of grace, that we may receive mercy and find grace to help in time of need." Hebrews 4:15-16*

Question 2. According to Hebrews 4:15, what does Jesus feel regarding our weaknesses?

_____

_____

_____

_____

Question 3. How does Hebrews 4:16 compare with what Jesus did for John and Mary while He was on the cross?

_____

_____

_____

_____

At Calvary, John and Mary *"drew near"* to Jesus, and there they received mercy and found grace to help them in their time of need. Mary was given a son to care for her and John, a mother who would love and care for him. Still today, Jesus helps all who draw near to Him because, on the cross, He purchased and secured for us all the grace, mercy, and help from God that we will ever need.

There is an old hymn titled **Moment by Moment** whose last verse describes the sympathy Jesus' has for us:

> *Never a weakness that He doth not feel,*
> *Never a sickness that He cannot heal;*
> *Moment by moment, in woe or in weal,*
> *Jesus my Savior, abides with me still.*

And the reason Jesus can not only feel our weaknesses and sympathize with us, but also save, heal, and deliver us, is His death on the cross. The hymn writer knew this too and made it the foundation of the song in the first stanza:

> *Dying with Jesus, by death reckoned mine;*
> *Living with Jesus, a new life divine;*
> *Looking to Jesus till glory doth shine,*
> *Moment by moment, O Lord, I am Thine.*[39]

Because Jesus Christ died for us, and we died in Him, He can heal, save, and abide with us. Jesus sympathizes with us in our weak flesh, but He doesn't just

---

39   https://hymnary.org/text/dying_with_jesus_by_death_reckoned_mine

feel bad for us; by His wounds, He heals us (1 Peter 2:24). He purchased our healing on the cross. Oh, what love and care Jesus has for us! It is powerful; it changes us from the inside out.

> *"This is how we know what love is: Jesus Christ laid down his life for us. And we ought to lay down our lives for our brothers and sisters." 1 John 3:16 NIV*

We noted earlier that Jesus provided for His mother through John. And this is the way of Jesus' love; it compels us to love and care for others. Note how the Apostle Paul commanded the church to exhibit the same love and care for each other:

> *"...encourage him as you would a father, younger men as brothers, older women as mothers, younger women as sisters, in all purity. Honor widows who are truly widows." 1 Timothy 5:1-3*

Question 4. How does the instruction Paul gave in 1 Timothy 5:1-3 compare with the love and care Jesus demonstrated on the cross for his mother?

_____

_____

_____

_____

Paul instructed Timothy to love, care for, and provide for his congregation as if they were family, because they are. We believers are an eternal family. For Jesus' sake, we are to show genuine affection for each other, and special attention is given to widows. Jesus' mother was a widow, and Jesus made sure to make provision for her before He died, and His desire was fulfilled by John, who *"from that hour...took her (Mary) into his home"* (John 19:27).

Paul gave broader but similar instructions in Romans 12:9-11:

"Let love be genuine. Abhor what is evil; hold fast to what is good.[10] Love one another with brotherly affection. Outdo one another in showing honor.[11] Do not be slothful in zeal, be fervent in spirit, serve the Lord." Romans 12:9-11

Question 5. Paul's instructions to the Romans, among other things, was for them to "love one another with brotherly affection" and to "outdo one another in showing honor." How did Jesus Christ do both of these things while on the cross?

_____

_____

_____

_____

Peter also spoke to this same cross of Christ compelling love for each other, *"Having purified your souls by your obedience to the truth for a sincere brotherly love, love one another earnestly from a pure heart,"* 1 Peter 1:22

Question 6. According to 1 Peter 1:22, what essential ingredient precedes being able to love others earnestly, as Jesus did on the cross?

_____

_____

_____

_____

Purity precedes godly passion. This biblical principle is an essential truth for all who follow Christ and earnestly desire to look like Christ. When we come to Jesus for cleansing by His blood, we are obedient to the gospel and empowered by God's Holy Spirit to love others sincerely from a pure heart.

Jesus Christ obeyed His Father in all things, and most significantly through His death, Jesus evidenced that He loved His family (both temporary and eternal) earnestly and sincerely. The cross teaches us what brotherly, earnest, and sincere love is. It is caring for others, being interested in their well-being, making provision for them, and putting their interests ahead of our own. Pure and sincere love for others is thinking of others and serving them even when we are in hardship. It is supernatural, cross-focused, Spirit-empowered love!

The cross is God's pledge to love, care for, and meet the needs of all who come to Him. By our coming to the cross in these studies, we have heard Jesus pray words of forgiveness for His enemies, speak words of life and hope to the thief dying beside Him, and now we have listened and learned from Jesus' words of love and care for His mother who stood by Him in His hour of death. May God enable us to cleanse ourselves at the cross of Christ, honor our parents, and love our brothers and sisters in Christ sincerely from pure hearts, for His glory.

Question 7. Please share any final thoughts or questions about this lesson:

_____

_____

_____

_____

Qynne writes, "*I am so falling in love with my Savior all over again! Thank you for helping me turn my gaze upon His loveliness.*"

Shay writes, "*I have just come from reading a critique of Christianity on an Islamic apologetics website, which pointed out "contradictions" and unresolved issues of the Bible. One of the things that stood out was that they said Christ was substituted on the cross, and so escaped. Since this was in direct opposition to the truth I learn here, I meditated on what might happen* *if this did happen. I saw no future for my soul or me, nor for any reason to love or cherish those things I hold dear. I saw no personal relationship with God. I only saw the demanding quite unmerciful face of Allah, to whom compromise is a luxury that he bestows on his faithful who lie and kill in his name. I saw a long blackness in which neither is hope nor peace. Needless to say, I thanked and praised God for reconciling me to Him with the cross, and in particular, to the love that I have now from Him with a pure heart, the very heart of worship to God."*

LESSON 27:

Words of Distress that Bring Us Peace

In these past few lessons, we have been standing at the foot of the cross and listening to the final words spoken by our Beloved Jesus, leaning in, as it were, to hear His final thoughts before He gave up His Spirit and died. We have been encouraged by the last words of forgiveness, acceptance, hope, life, love, and care that Jesus prayed and spoke. But now, we have come to Christ's pinnacle of pain. At this point in the narrative, most want to turn and run from what they see and hear, the sorrow is too palpable, but if we stay and keep listening, we will find that these words of Jesus, though filled with misery and torment, also translate to words of promise for us who believe. Hear the words of your Lord:

> *And about the ninth hour Jesus cried out with a loud voice, saying, "Eli, Eli, lema sabachthani?" that is, "My God, my God, why have you forsaken me?" Matthew 27:46*

Years ago, after my wife gave birth to our twin daughters, she was struck with Bell's palsy, which caused pain and paralysis on the left side of her face. She no longer looked like herself because the functioning muscles in her face pulled while the weak side of her face yielded. When she went out in public, people would quickly avert their gaze when they saw the distortion of her face. And while she understood their discomfort, it was hurtful to experience the revulsion of strangers for something over which she had no control. Because of my love for her, my heart suffered along with her. This small suffering we can comprehend, but how can we even articulate the momentous moment where God forsook His *"beloved Son"* in whom He was well pleased?

SETTING CAPTIVES FREE

Jesus hung on His cross, distorted not by His sins but by the sins of the whole world—past, present, and future—by your sins and mine, and it was not strangers that turned away from Him, but His Father with Whom He had enjoyed eternal fellowship since before the world began.

Previously Jesus had prayed, "Father, forgive..." but now He cries out, *"My God, my God!"* Jesus became sin on the cross, and keenly felt the broken fellowship with the Father as a result. He no longer prays to His Father; now He cries out in torment, "My God!" His agony is beyond our understanding.

But God, the Father, did not turn away from Jesus because of personal discomfort. It was not as if Jesus were just something unpleasant to see. God had to turn away from Jesus because God is holy! God is so holy that He *"cannot look on sin"* (Habakkuk 1:13). And because God is holy, He cannot allow sin to go unpunished for that would not be holy or righteous. God rightly demands justice for all sin committed, and Romans 6:23 tells us that all sin merits *death*.

But death is not the mere cessation of life; death is separation. Physical death is the separation of the soul from the body. Spiritual death is the separation of the soul from God. Physical and Spiritual death was the necessary payment for our sin, which is why Jesus had to die physically, and God had to sever His connection with Jesus temporarily.

The prophet Nahum asked the question, *"Who can stand before His indignation? And who can abide in the fierceness of His anger?"* (Nahum 1:6). From the cross, the answer resounds, "Jesus can!"

Jesus alone can *"stand."* Only He could bear the curse of the Law and endure the agonies of physical and spiritual death, and rise victorious. Only He could suffer all the wrath of a Holy God and, while doing so, magnify the Law and make it honorable. Only He could let His "heel" be bruised by Satan and in that bruising *destroy him* (the devil) that had the power of death.

Oh, friend, Jesus was *forsaken* by God, *alienated* from Him, *rejected* and *abandoned* by Him to atone for our sin.

God is not only the embodiment of justice, holiness, and righteousness, but He is also perfect love! He delights in mercy, and therefore in His wisdom, He devised a way that justice might be satisfied and mercy might flow freely to those who sin. This way was the cross, the method of substitution, the Just suffering for the unjust.

On that "midnight at midday" (as Pastor Charles Spurgeon called it), a divine transaction occurred. Our Representative, Jesus, became sin for us. He took our place on the cross, bore our sins in His own body, drank the full cup of God's wrath, was despised and rejected by men and forsaken of God. And as He hung there, cursed, afflicted, abandoned, and rejected by God, the miraculous happened; God in Christ reconciled the world to Himself, "*not counting men's sins against them!*" *(2 Corinthians 5:19)*.

God the Father forsook His Son temporarily that we might enjoy fellowship with Him forever. He poured out His wrath on Christ so that we would be saved from it *through* Christ. God does not treat us as our sins deserve because He treated Jesus as our sins deserve!

The question Jesus cried out in anguish, *"My God, my God, why have you forsaken Me?"* we can answer. Jesus' cries of anguish purchased our tears of joy and cries of thankfulness! Jesus entered the dark and dreadful storm of God's wrath that we might be set free to enjoy the Light (Job 33:28). His abandonment is our acceptance (Ephesians 1:6). He was forsaken that we might be forgiven; He was despised that we might be loved!

Such good news! The only appropriate response to Jesus' horrible suffering on our behalf is our *worship, thanksgiving, and praise.*

> *"And they sang a new song, saying, "Worthy are you to take the scroll and to open its seals, for you were slain, and by your blood you ransomed people for God from every tribe and language and people and nation," Revelation 5:9*

Oh, friend, I pray that your heart is singing the song of the redeemed along with me! We are a ransomed, blood-bought Bride richly blessed in Jesus!

Let us never forget these final words of torment our Savior cried as He hung on the cross paying the wages of our sin! Let us preach, pray, and sing the gospel to ourselves and each other daily, for unless we do, we will give in to either despair or pride, both of which are death to the soul. Let us be those who love to both hear and tell the story of Jesus. As the old hymn says:

> *Tell of the cross where they nailed Him,*
> *Writhing in anguish and pain.*

Tell of the grave where they laid Him,
Tell how He liveth again.
Love in that story so tender,
Clearer than ever I see.
Stay, let me weep while you whisper,
Love paid the ransom for me.[40]

Question 1. What is your response to the cry of anguish from the lips of Jesus Christ on the cross?

_____

_____

_____

_____

Bill writes, *"This aspect of the cross is mind-boggling in its enormity. I believe that the most excruciatingly painful thing Jesus suffered on the cross was the inevitable and unavoidable separation from the Father, an occurrence that had never happened prior to that moment and will never happen again! And the fact that Jesus and the Father were willing to cause and endure this occurrence is astonishing. My finite mind cannot grasp it, but I most humbly and gratefully accept it as a sacrifice pleasing to the Father, by which Jesus made a way for me to be reconciled to the Father and have eternal life. Praise You, and blessed be Your Name, my Lord Jesus, my Liberator, my Regenerator, my All-in-All!!!"*

Let's finish up this lesson affirming the same truth that Charles Spurgeon did:

"I will tell you this thing about myself to encourage you. My sole hope for heaven lies in the full atonement made upon Calvary's

---

40   https://hymnary.org/text/tell_me_the_story_of_jesus_write_on_my_h

cross for the ungodly. On that I firmly rely. I have not the shadow of a hope anywhere else. You are in the same condition as I am; for we neither of us have anything of our own worth as a ground of trust. Let us join hands and stand together at the foot of the cross, and trust our souls once for all to Him who shed His blood for the guilty. We will be saved by one and the same Saviour. If you perish trusting Him, I must perish too. What can I do more to prove my own confidence in the gospel which I set before you?"[41]

41   https://ccel.org/ccel/spurgeon/grace/grace.vi.html

LESSON 28:

Words of Suffering that
Satisfy Us

*I*n recent lessons, we have been considering Jesus' final words from the cross. We have heard our Savior speak words of forgiveness, life, hope, love, care, and agony from His cross. We've understood these words of His were intentional and that they hold deep meaning for all who believe.

The cross of Christ stands as a lasting memorial to the forgiveness, abundant life, eternal hope, immeasurable love, compassionate care, and full acceptance with God that we have through the death and resurrection of our Jesus! In today's lesson, we will hear two words that articulate Jesus' suffering to bring many sons and daughters to glory (Hebrews 2:10).

> *"After this, Jesus, knowing that all was now finished, said (to fulfill the Scripture), "I thirst." John 19:28*

Jesus' words on the cross, "I thirst," are multi-faceted, and it is right that we take the time to consider and understand the varied aspects of them.

First, Jesus' thirst was literal. In the Garden of Gethsemane, Jesus was so distraught that His sweat was like *"great drops of blood,"* then he lost a lot of blood because of the whipping from the Roman soldiers, and it had been hours since He had had anything to drink. Due to prolonged stress, blood loss, and physical abuse, Jesus' body was dehydrated, and he was physically thirsty. As humans, we can all relate, on some level, to the ache of Jesus' physical thirst.

Second, John tells us that Jesus said, *"I thirst"* *"to fulfill the Scripture."* Here are two such Scriptures which Jesus' fulfilled:

"My strength is dried up like baked clay; my tongue sticks to the roof of my mouth. You put me into the dust of death." Psalms 22:15 (HCSB)

"Instead, they gave me gall for my food, and for my thirst they gave me vinegar to drink." Psalms 69:21 (HCSB)

Jesus Christ upheld the Scriptures perfectly in His life and His death. He spoke words, *"I thirst"* as another proof that He was the Promised Messiah of which the Scriptures spoke.

The Old Testament contains hundreds of prophecies about the promised Messiah, and Jesus fulfilled them all. His suffering was planned with the Father and the Spirit before time began, and Jesus deliberately gave Himself to it for our sakes. *"He suffered death so that by the grace of God, he might taste death for everyone." Hebrews 2:9* Jesus was never a victim; He was fully conscious and in control of His situation at all times. Isn't it incredible that, on the cross, Jesus tasted death for everyone, but had not a drop of water offered to Him?

Finally, we can see that Jesus' words, *"I thirst,"* evidence that He fully entered into our sinful condition as He hung on the cross. Though He was sinless, holy, pure, and perfect, on the cross, He had *"become sin for us"* that we might *"become the righteousness of God in Him"* (2 Corinthians 5:21).

The Bible gives us many word-pictures for the condition of humanity apart from Christ. A few examples are: "lost" (Luke 15:4), "trapped" (Psalm 59:2; Isaiah 42:22; Proverbs 5:22), "captives" (Luke 4:18; 2 Timothy 2:25-26), "enemies of God", (James 4:4), "dead in sins" (Ephesians 2:1-3) and "thirsty." By the word "thirsty," we understand the Bible to mean we are by nature "unsatisfied," "craving," "yearning," and "longing." This concept is easily understood when we consider a conversation Jesus had with a woman at a well in Samaria. Let's read it together from John 4.

"A woman from Samaria came to draw water. Jesus said to her, "Give me a drink."[8] (For his disciples had gone away into the city to buy food.)" John 4:7-8

Notice that Jesus initiated this conversation with the woman at the well. Previously the Bible tells us that Jesus *"had to go through Samaria"* (John 4:4), which was unlike typical Jews of that day who loathed the Samaritans and always tried to go *around* Samaria when going to Galilee. But Jesus came to *"seek and to save the lost"* and rescue men and women from the trap of the devil (2 Timothy 2:25-26), so He went to Samaria to meet with this woman.

Now, Jesus was thirsty from his journey, so he asked this woman for a drink of water. The woman was astonished that Jesus spoke to her for two reasons. First, in those days, Jews did not usually associate with Samaritans but despised them, and second, women were thought to be inferior to men and treated as such. And so, in surprise, the woman answered Jesus with a question of her own:

> *"The Samaritan woman said to him, "How is it that you, a Jew, ask for a drink from me, a woman of Samaria?" (For Jews have no dealings with Samaritans.)" John 4:9*

Jesus was clearly different from any other man this woman had ever met. Jesus ignored both the racial and gender biases of His day to meet this woman's eternal need. As we will see later, most men in this woman's life only took from her and then left her empty and used, but Jesus would give to her, satisfy her soul, and leave her with so much that she had some to share with others. He did for this woman what He would later do on the cross for us. Jesus used His own "thirst" as a starting point to quench the thirst of others.

> *"Jesus answered her, "If you knew the gift of God, and who it is that is saying to you, 'Give me a drink,' you would have asked him, and he would have given you living water." John 4:10*

Jesus had *"living water,"* yet He asked this woman for a drink. Here we see Jesus presenting Himself to a Samaritan woman as One Who could quench her thirst, but she doesn't understand what He means because she responds with the following:

"Sir, you have nothing to draw water with, and the well is deep. Where do you get that living water?[12] *Are you greater than our father Jacob? He gave us the well and drank from it himself, as did his sons and his livestock."" John 4:11-12*

Question 1. Does this woman presently have a proper view of Who Jesus Christ is? Please explain:

_____

_____

_____

_____

This Samaritan woman does not yet understand Who Jesus is. She doesn't know that Jesus is indeed much greater than her forefather, Jacob. Thirst, or *longing in the soul,* is always due to misunderstanding Who Jesus is and living apart from Him.

"Jesus said to her, "Everyone who drinks of this water will be thirsty again,[14] *but whoever drinks of the water that I will give him will never be thirsty again. The water that I will give him will become in him a spring of water welling up to eternal life." John 4:13-14*

Question 2. Please examine John 4:13-14. What are the different kinds of "water" listed in these verses? Compare and contrast the different kinds of water. What is said about each?

_____

_____

_____

_____

We notice from this passage that there are two kinds of water listed:

"*This water...*" and "*the water that I will give.*"

"This water" refers to the physical water, the water that was in the well. Jesus said that whoever drank "this water" would be thirsty again. That is obvious; it makes sense. We may quench our thirst with water today, but we find that we get thirsty again tomorrow and must drink again.

So, it follows that "*The water I will give*" must be an entirely different kind of water. Jesus said that the person who drinks the water He would give would never be thirsty again. Wow! That must be some water for it to quench our thirst eternally. To what is Jesus referring here? The next verses give us the key to understanding this passage:

> "*The woman said to him, "Sir, give me this water, so that I will not be thirsty or have to come here to draw water."[16] Jesus said to her, "Go, call your husband, and come here."[17] The woman answered him, "I have no husband." Jesus said to her, "You are right in saying, 'I have no husband'; 18 for you have had five husbands, and the one you now have is not your husband. What you have said is true." John 4:15-18*

Question 3. According to John 4:18, how many husbands had this woman at the well had in her life?

_____

_____

_____

_____

Question 4. What does the woman's marital status have to do with drinking water and Jesus' offer to quench her thirst? Why did Jesus bring up the issue of her past marriages?

_____

_____

This issue of "thirsting again" when drinking *"this water"* ("water" of this world) is directly tied in with the woman's past marital failures. Can you see the connection? Jesus did not randomly switch subjects when speaking with this woman. He did not arbitrarily go from discussing water to relationships. He is making a connection between the two for this woman and us.

The Samaritan woman was thirsty and not just physically. She was thirsty spiritually but attempting to quench her thirst, that is, satisfy her longing, in physical relationships. Over the years, she had undoubtedly discovered that as she continued to "drink" of one relationship after another, she was never fully satisfied, that is, her thirst was never really quenched. *"Whoever drinks this water will be thirsty again."*

In this woman's life story, we see the biblical terminology for "addiction." The biblical phrase that describes "addiction" is to be *"thirsty again."* The person who turns to alcohol, cigarettes, pornography, food, sinful relationships, money, man's approval, etc. to fill a void within them, soon discovers that once is not enough. They must have another "drink" and another. They must search for more pornography with which to gratify the lusts of their flesh. They must have another cigarette, another donut, another dollar because there is never total satisfaction within their soul. Sin is dehydrating to the soul, leaving one's soul a barren desert.

Pastor Richard Blanchard summed up this relentless thirsting of our flesh well when he wrote the hymn, *Fill My Cup, Lord.* The first lines of the song are: *"Like the woman at the well, I was seeking, For things that could not satisfy..."* [42]

And it is this very thirst in the soul that Jesus entered into on the cross. He was not merely physically thirsty, but when He *"became sin for us,"* He came into the painful human condition of *"thirsting."*

But unlike our thirst, Jesus' suffering in thirst was purposeful and powerful. Jesus thirsted on the cross that we might become satisfied in Him. He became parched that we might become quenched. What a Savior!

Think of it: the Maker of Heaven and earth with parched lips, the Lord of glory in need of a drink. Jesus offered up His soul to become a barren desert,

---

42   https://www.hymnal.net/en/hymn/ns/340

as He poured out His life unto death so that our souls might become like the Jordan valley *"well-watered everywhere, like the Lord's garden" (Genesis 13:10)*!

Because of Jesus, there is an answer to the human condition of "thirsting" and a solution for our endless "drinking" that never satisfies. Jesus said to the woman at the well, *"He who drinks the water I give him will never thirst."* Ahh, here is the cure for "addiction," biblically known as "thirsting." The cure for addiction is not merely stopping the troublesome behavior, but instead, it is to drink the "water" Jesus gives so that our thirst might be quenched.

As Pastor Blanchard wrote, *"And then I heard my Savior speaking; "Draw from My well that never shall run dry,,,"*[43]

By the end of her time with Jesus, the Samaritan woman at the well understood the analogy. She got the word-picture. How do we know this? Look at this:

> *"So the woman left her water jar and went away into town and said to the people,*[29] *"Come, see a man who told me all that I ever did. Can this be the Christ?"" John 4:28-29*

Question 5. What did the woman at the well do with her water jar?

_____

_____

_____

_____

Question 6. When she went into the town of Samaria, what message did she have to share with others?

_____

_____

_____

_____

---

43   https://www.hymnal.net/en/hymn/ns/340

The woman left her water jar with Jesus. Why? Well, we can certainly imagine that she was in a hurry to tell others about Jesus. After all, He promised to quench her thirst, that is, satisfy the longings in her soul. But I don't think it is a stretch of the imagination to say that this woman had begun drinking the excellent life-giving water of Jesus already. As she understood that Jesus used *"this water"* as a symbol of her attempts to quench her thirst in sinful ways, she now repented and left her waterpot behind.

My friend, I wonder, is there any of *"this water"* in your life right now? Are you thirsting after something, pursuing someone or something that does not truly quench your thirst? If so, isn't it time to "leave your water pot" with Jesus?

> *"So, brother, if the things this world gave you,*
> *Leave hungers that won't pass away;*
> *My blessed Lord will come and save you;*
> *If you kneel to Him and humbly pray."*[44]

As we consider these words Jesus cried out in His final moments on the cross, we learn much from these two words, *"I thirst."* We discover His humanity evidenced in His physical thirst, the intensity of His sufferings, His fulfillment of the prophetic Scriptures, and His full submission to the Father's will. And more intimately, we understand how Christ, who knew no sin, can sympathize with our sufferings with sin because, on the cross, He entered into our "thirst." We are born "thirsters," and until our thirst is quenched in Jesus, we will continue searching for satisfaction in sinful relationships, alcohol, work, or any other false water fountains.

Question 7. How is it with you today? Do you recognize that Jesus thirsted on the cross to quench your own thirst? Are you drinking (receiving grace and finding satisfaction) from Jesus?

44   https://www.hymnal.net/en/hymn/ns/340

_____

_____

Candy writes, *"Yes, I see how Jesus thirsted so that I would no longer be thirsty. Because of His grace, I can say that Jesus is quenching that thirst I once had. I have come so far since starting these lessons on the Cross. I have struggled with my walk with the Lord for a long time. But even though at times, I felt close to the Lord, I have never known what I know about Jesus today. I am so grateful for these lessons and how the Lord is opening my mind and heart to receive His Word. The last few weeks of doing these lessons have been the most satisfying in my life. Now I can honestly say that I do not thirst as I once did."*

If you are still thirsting, may God open your eyes to the fountain of living water that is just a prayer away. If you are quenching your thirst in Jesus, then your future is described in these verses from Revelation:

"Therefore they are before the throne of God, and serve him day and night in his temple; and he who sits on the throne will shelter them with his presence. [16] They shall hunger no more, neither thirst anymore; the sun shall not strike them, nor any scorching heat. [17] For the Lamb in the midst of the throne will be their shepherd, and he will guide them to springs of living water, and God will wipe away every tear from their eyes." Revelation 7:15-17

Words of Triumph

*I*n these past several lessons, we have come together to the foot of Jesus' cross to *"Behold the Lamb"* that takes away our sin, where we have leaned in and listened to the final words of our Beloved. Our hearts have been both cut by the sufferings of Jesus for our sins (Acts 2:37) and healed by the wounds of Jesus (1 Peter 2:24), which bring us peace (Isaiah 53:5). We have been encouraged and taught by Jesus' prayer for forgiveness and built up in our faith by His words of life, hope, love, and care. We found acceptance and thirst-quenching satisfaction through His words of suffering, *"My God, My God, why have you forsaken me?"* and *"I thirst."* And now, we hear the long-awaited words from our Lord, not whispered or mumbled in defeat, but shouted out in triumph:

> *"When he had received the drink, Jesus said, "It is finished." With that, he bowed his head and gave up his spirit." John 19:30*

Usually, at the end of life, a person's voice gets softer and quieter, but despite all that He had suffered for hours on the cross, the gospel of Mark records that Jesus uttered a loud cry (Mark 15:37) before He died! Most likely this is when Jesus yelled out the word, "Tetelestai!" meaning *"It is finished!"* as a cry of victory, a declaration of success and completion.

As we contemplate this final word of triumph from Jesus, to truly benefit from it we must understand what it is that Jesus finished; and, as we do, we will *"grow in the grace and knowledge of our Lord and Savior Jesus Christ."* The truth about Jesus' finished work will strengthen our hearts and stabilize our lives (2 Peter 3:17-18).

Facing his own death, the prophet John the Baptist discovered the strengthening power of Christ's work. We read in Luke 7:20-22, *"John the Baptist has sent us to you, saying, 'Are you the one who is to come, or shall we look for another?'" In that hour he healed many people of diseases and plagues and evil spirits, and on many who were blind he bestowed sight. And he answered them, "Go and tell John what you have seen and heard: the blind receive their sight, the lame walk, lepers are cleansed, and the deaf hear, the dead are raised up, the poor have good news preached to them."*

John the Baptist needed reassurance, and Jesus compassionately sent the ultimate word of encouragement—the fulfillment of the Scriptures about the Messiah.

Friend, Jesus has fulfilled all the Scriptures. *It is finished!* To name only a few, Jesus was born of a virgin, the seed of Abraham, of the lineage of David, born in Bethlehem in Judea. In life, He opened the eyes of the blind and the ears of the deaf, made the lame walk, and the mute speak. He was despised and rejected by man and *"hated without a cause."* At the time of His death, Jesus was betrayed and deserted by all, falsely accused and wrongly condemned just as the Scriptures said He would be. He was mocked, and lots cast for His last piece of clothing. He was wounded, pierced, beaten and scourged according to the Scriptures. And finally, He suffered and died at the hands of evil men. All these Scriptures, and many more, were fulfilled by Jesus Christ when He died on the cross. Not one prophecy missed. *It is finished!*

> **Question 1.** How is your faith affected as you consider all the prophecies that Jesus fulfilled through His life and death on the cross?
>
> _____
>
> _____
>
> _____
>
> _____

The first prophecy of Christ is found in Genesis when God speaks to the serpent who deceived Eve:

"I will put enmity between you and the woman, and between your offspring and her offspring; he shall bruise your head, and you shall bruise his heel."

Question 2. How does Genesis 3:15 point forward to the cross?

_____

_____

_____

_____

The prophecy in Genesis 3 speaks of One to come who would stomp on the serpent's head and suffer in the process. The cross is the bite of the serpent, but also the fatal blow to the devil.

On the surface, the cross looked like the devil's greatest triumph and Christ's ultimate failure, but, in reality, things were exactly opposite of what they appeared. Jesus made this statement earlier, before His death, and because of the upcoming cross:

> *"Now is the judgment of this world; now will the ruler of this world be cast out." John 12:31*

While the devil has not yet been chained and cast into the bottomless pit, his doom is sure. Jesus has broken Satan's power over us. As John wrote, *"Little children, you are from God and have overcome them, for he who is in you is greater than he who is in the world."* 1 John 4:4

In his hymn, *A Mighty Fortress*, Martin Luther put it this way:

> *And though this world, with devils filled,*
> *should threaten to undo us,*
> *we will not fear, for God hath willed*
> *his truth to triumph through us.*
> *The Prince of Darkness grim,*

we tremble not for him;
his rage we can endure,
for lo, his doom is sure;
one little word shall fell him.[45]

Jesus has *"destroyed him who had the power of death, that is, the devil"* (Hebrews *2:14*).

> **Question 3.** According to Hebrews 2:14, through His death on the cross, what did Jesus do to Satan?
>
> _____
>
> _____
>
> _____
>
> _____

Oh, how marvelous! The cross was like an upside-down sword, plunged into the heart of the devil, and now he is a defeated foe, and we are certain victors through the cross. *"It is finished!"*

Not only did Jesus finish the work of crushing Satan, but He also removed the curse of the law from us.

The Law of God commanded perfection or death. It was not complicated to understand, but our problem was that, because of the weakness of our flesh (see Romans 8:1-4), we couldn't obey. Because of our sinful human condition, we could never fulfill the law as we should. But the good news is that what we could not do, Jesus, our Savior, did it for us!

> *"For God has done what the law, weakened by the flesh, could not do. By sending his own Son in the likeness of sinful flesh and for sin, he condemned sin in the flesh, in order that the righteous requirement of the law might be fulfilled in us, who walk not according to the flesh but according to the Spirit." Romans 8:3-4*

45   https://hymnary.org/text/a_mighty_fortress_is_our_god_a_bulwark

Question 4. According to Romans 8:3-4, what did Christ accomplish in us?

_____

_____

_____

_____

Romans 8 tells us that the law's requirements have been accomplished in us by Christ. Oh, let this reality sink into your heart and mind! God views each of His children as having fulfilled the righteous requirements of the law perfectly in His Son! He sees me, and you, if you believe, as having lived a perfect life, as sinless and spotless (Colossians 1:22), having obeyed the law down to its smallest jot and tittle.

Those who want to put people back under the Mosaic law are called "Judaizers" and "legalists" in the Bible. Scripture defines them as those who eat special diets for religious reasons and who keep "special days" (Romans 14:1-7; Galatians 4:8-11). Sadly, these legalists do not understand the inflexible demands of the law (perfection) or the horrible consequences of disobeying even a tiny portion of it (eternal death!). They do not understand that they, themselves, are under a curse:

> *"For all who rely on works of the law are under a curse; for it is written, "Cursed be everyone who does not abide by all things written in the Book of the Law, and do them." Galatians 3:10*

Through His perfect life, Jesus Christ *fulfilled the demands* of the law for all who believe (Matthew 5:17), *and* through His substitutionary death, He *removed the curse* of the law for us. Oh, how this should move our souls to praise Him, Who died for us!

Hymn writer Philip Bliss was rejoicing in this truth when he wrote the lyrics, *"Free from the Law, O happy condition! Jesus hath bled, and there is remission, Cursed by the law and dead by the fall, Grace hath redeemed us, once and for all."*[46]

---

46   https://hymnary.org/text/free_from_the_law_o_happy_condition

Are you beginning to grasp why Jesus yelled out His victory cry? On the cross, Jesus was at war, and He won! The cross was the culmination of a lifetime of perfect obedience for our sakes. His single word from the cross, meaning *"It is finished!"* is life-transforming for us because it set us free from the power of sin and the law (see 1 Corinthians 15:55-56)!

Isaiah 53:10-12 gives us a fuller understanding of Jesus' work on the cross:

> *"Yet it was the will of the Lord to crush him; he has put him to grief; when his soul makes an offering for guilt, he shall see his offspring; he shall prolong his days; the will of the Lord shall prosper in his hand. Out of the anguish of his soul he shall see and be satisfied; by his knowledge shall the righteous one, my servant, make many to be accounted righteous, and he shall bear their iniquities. Therefore I will divide him a portion with the many, and he shall divide the spoil with the strong, because he poured out his soul to death and was numbered with the transgressors; yet he bore the sin of many, and makes intercession for the transgressors."*

Question 5. According to Isaiah 53:10-12, what was the work Jesus was given to do?

_____

_____

_____

_____

Before Christ came to this earth, a specific job was entrusted to Him. He was to be crushed, put to grief, an offering, the bearer of our sins, poured out to death for us. When we put our faith in Jesus' sacrifice of His own body on the cross, we are counted as righteous!

Hebrews 10:4-5 tells us, *"For it is impossible for the blood of bulls and goats to take away sins. Consequently, when Christ came into the world, he said, "Sacrifices and offerings you have not desired, but a body have you prepared for me..."*

Jesus' final word of victory, *"It is finished!"* assures us that His offering was completed on our behalf. Our sins have been atoned through Jesus who did God's will perfectly! God's wrath for our sin has been satisfied by the blood offering of the perfect Lamb of God, His own Son. Hebrews 10:10 confirms, *"And by that will we have been sanctified through the offering of the body of Jesus Christ once for all."*

> **Question 6.** According to Hebrews 10:10, what happened to us through Jesus' offering on the cross?
>
> _____
>
> _____
>
> _____
>
> _____

We have been sanctified through Jesus, dear friend! We were born in sin, but through Jesus, we have been born again into a new life set apart from the power of sin.

Through Daniel, the Holy Spirit prophesied of the cleansing and sanctifying work of Jesus:

> *"Seventy weeks are decreed about your people and your holy city, to finish the transgression, to put an end to sin, and to atone for iniquity, to bring in everlasting righteousness, to seal both vision and prophet, and to anoint a most holy place." Daniel 9:24*

Jesus was sent to *put an end to sin*, to *atone* for our sins, to *bring in eternal righteousness* for us, and He did it all by dying sacrificially on the cross. When Christ died, all the sins of His people died with Him. When Jesus died, our sins were dealt a death-blow. No believer will ever have to answer for one sin as our sins have already been answered for, removed from us, and annihilated in the Person and work of Jesus Christ. Jesus "finished transgression" and "put an end to sin" when He said, "It is finished!"

When Jesus died, *"the Lord laid on Him the iniquity of us all"* (Isaiah 53:6).

And since God laid our iniquities on Christ, they are no longer on "us all." Jesus had no sin *in* Him but had sin placed *on* Him, and while sin remains in us because of our flesh, there is never sin *on* us because of Christ's sacrifice. There is no condemnation for those in Christ (Romans 8:1); we are free from all accusation (Colossians 1:22) because all our sin, along with its guilt, shame, and blame, was transferred to our Substitute, Jesus!

Question 7. According to Isaiah 53:6, what happened to all our sin?

_____

_____

_____

_____

We, believers, are blessed beyond measure in our Lord Jesus! Our enemy Satan has been defeated. Satan's weapon of death has been destroyed through Jesus' death on the cross and victorious resurrection! The law of God has been fulfilled for us by Jesus; there is no longer any curse or condemnation for us in Christ. Jesus has made atonement for our sins; we are eternally safe in Him. Our sins are gone, erased as if they never existed! Jesus' work is finished, but our experience of it will never end. Throughout eternity, we will be singing the praises of our Beloved, who gave Himself for us to redeem, ransom, and rescue us from sin, death, hell, and God's justice. *"It is finished!"*

Question 8. Please share any thoughts about the lesson today.

_____

_____

_____

_____

Derick writes, *"I always heard and even read the scriptures in John 19:30 that declares, "It is finished!" But because of today's lesson, I finally understand it! I can see what and how it was finished. It is so amazing what God sent His Son to do, but it is so much more amazing that Jesus loved His assignment so much that He finished it with power. I am so grateful!"*

LESSON 30:

Confident Words of Peace

We come now to our seventh and final lesson on Jesus' last words. We've drawn near to the cross, leaned in, listened, sorrowed, and rejoiced, considering the final words of our Savior. Today, as we listen to the final words of Jesus, we will learn how applying the cross of Christ to our life changes everything for us, including death.

On the night of His betrayal, Jesus went to the Garden of Gethsemane with His disciples. They went there to pray, but the disciples in their weakness could only sleep. So, Jesus poured out His heart alone. His anguish was so intense that His sweat became like drops of blood, but there was no one to comfort Him or wipe His brow in His time of need. Three times Jesus woke the disciples, but they had no words of consolation for Him (Mark 14:40). Finally, Jesus said, *"Are you still sleeping and taking your rest? It is enough; the hour has come. The Son of Man is betrayed into the hands of sinners. Rise, let us be going; see, my betrayer is at hand."* Mark 14:41 And Mark records that immediately Jesus was betrayed by Judas, abandoned by His disciples, seized, and taken before the high priest.

Jesus was betrayed *"into the hands of sinners"* not reluctantly but intentionally. He woke His disciples saying, "Let's go!" He went to meet His betrayer as One eager to answer the call on His life. Jesus committed to the agonies and abuse of the cross for us, His Bride, as eagerly as Jacob worked for His beloved Rachel (Genesis 29:21-30). In the Garden of Gethsemane, Jesus committed Himself *into the hands of sinners* to do the work He was sent to do—the atoning, saving, sanctifying, life-transforming, love-displaying work of Calvary!

But after Jesus finished the work He had to do on the cross, there were new hands to receive Him. Hands that Jesus had trusted before the foundations of the world.

"Then Jesus, calling out with a loud voice, said, "Father, into your hands I commit my spirit!" And having said this he breathed his last." Luke 23:46

Can you feel the calm strength and the confident control of our Lord at this moment? There is no slipping away quietly for our Savior. He is the Hero willingly giving His life to rescue us, His damsel in distress! And, as the victor, He committed His Spirit into the hands of the Father who loved Him and approved of the beautiful, glorious, saving, and sanctifying work He had done.

"For this reason the Father loves me, because I lay down my life that I may take it up again. No one takes it from me, but I lay it down of my own accord. I have authority to lay it down, and I have authority to take it up again. This charge I have received from my Father." John 10:17-18

Question 1. According to John 10:17-18, why does the Father love the Son?

_____

_____

_____

_____

The Father, Son, and Spirit were in loving agreement about the necessary means to save us and make us a Bride fit for a King. They each had a part to play in our redemption, and They executed Their plan flawlessly. As always, They worked in perfect harmony doing all that They said They would. The Son was offered (Genesis 22:6-14), the Bride was created (Genesis 2:21-23), the way of restoration was forged (Isaiah 43:19), and eternal, perfect and sacrificial Love was enacted, displayed and proven (Hosea 3:1).

And, in consummate agreement and eternal joy, They have lavished their perfect love on us through the cross of Christ! *"See what kind of love the Father has given to us, that we should be called children of God; and so we are." 1 John 3:10*

The fact that Christ's life was not *taken*, but rather *given*, powerfully assures us of His eternal love for us. There is no greater love than this: *"that someone lay down His life for His friends" (John 15:13).*

> **Question 2.** How is your heart affected by the sacrificial love of Jesus, who willingly laid down His life for you?
>
> _____
>
> _____
>
> _____
>
> _____

In 1 John 3:16, we read the intended effect of Jesus' sacrificial love on us, *"By this, we know love, that he [Jesus] laid down his life for us, and we ought to lay down our lives for the brothers."* We should understand then that the love of Christ is not a love to be hoarded or consumed; it is a compelling love that we share with others, give away freely, and hand out to the undeserving like ourselves.

Paul spoke of Jesus' transforming love in his second letter to the Corinthians, *"For Christ's love compels us, because we are convinced that one died for all, and therefore all died. And he died for all, that those who live should no longer live for themselves but for him who died for them and was raised again. So from now on we regard no one from a worldly point of view. Though we once regarded Christ in this way, we do so no longer." 2 Corinthians 4:14-16*

Loving others sincerely and sacrificially, forgiving them as God has forgiven us, treating others not according to their flesh, but according to Christ, dying daily and living obediently to the gospel are all impossible apart from Christ and His cross.

Throughout this study, we have seen Jesus' death in our place, saving, atoning, and sanctifying us, but we must not miss the cross' guidance for our new and abundant life in Jesus. In these final words of Jesus on the cross, we find the way to live in His victory and to love others with His cross-focused love as we should.

Throughout His life, Jesus entrusted Himself to the One who judges justly (1 Peter 2:23), and in a final act of worship on His cross, Jesus entrusted Himself into the loving care of His Father, breathed out His last, and gave up His Spirit. We, too, can and should entrust ourselves and surrender our lives into the Father's hands.

Through the years, godly men and women have faced the trials of life by entrusting themselves into the hand of Almighty God, confident that He would rescue them from their distress through direct deliverance or death. We can see this bold reliance on God in the account of Shadrach, Meshach, and Abednego and the fiery furnace.

> *"Nebuchadnezzar answered and said to them, "Is it true, O Shadrach, Meshach, and Abednego, that you do not serve my gods or worship the golden image that I have set up? Now, if you are ready when you hear the sound of the horn, pipe, lyre, trigon, harp, bagpipe, and every kind of music, to fall down and worship the image that I have made, well and good. But if you do not worship, you shall immediately be cast into a burning fiery furnace. And who is the god who will deliver you out of my hands?" Shadrach, Meshach, and Abednego answered and said to the king, "O Nebuchadnezzar, we have no need to answer you in this matter. If this be so, our God, whom we serve, is able to deliver us from the burning fiery furnace, and he will deliver us out of your hand, O king. But if not, be it known to you, O king, that we will not serve your gods or worship the golden image that you have set up." Daniel 3:14-18*

These young men were in a dire situation—they were captives in Babylon with enemies plotting against them, facing a wrathful king and death by fire. And yet they put up no protest, no fight for their rights; they only expressed faith in God. They entrusted themselves to the true God, who saves and sets His people free. And, indeed, God did save them. King Nebuchanzer was astonished when he saw four men in the fire, and the fourth looked like the Son of God. The only thing that burned up in the fire was the rope that previously bound the Hebrew men.

"The hair of their heads was not singed, their cloaks were not harmed, and no smell of fire had come upon them. Nebuchadnezzar answered and said, "Blessed be the God of Shadrach, Meshach, and Abednego, who has sent his angel and delivered his servants, who trusted in him, and set aside the king's command, and yielded up their bodies rather than serve and worship any god except their own God." Daniel 3:27-28

Another example is King David, who learned to trust in God and even sang about it. Notice the foreshadowing of the death of Christ in this Psalm of David:

"In you, O Lord, do I take refuge; let me never be put to shame; in your righteousness, deliver me!² Incline your ear to me; rescue me speedily! Be a rock of refuge for me, a strong fortress to save me!³For you are my rock and my fortress, and for your name's sake you lead me and guide me;⁴you take me out of the net they have hidden for me, for you are my refuge.⁵Into your hand, I commit my spirit; you have redeemed me, O Lord, faithful God." Psalms 31:1-5

Question 3. According to Psalm 31:4, what were the conditions that David was facing as he penned this Psalm?

_____

_____

_____

_____

Question 4. According to Psalm 31:5, what did David do when facing this difficulty?

_____

_____

Question 5. According to Psalm 31:5, what was David's confident expectation as to the outcome of his trial?

King David rightly entrusted Himself into the care of God, confident that God would rescue him from those who plotted against him. And God did deliver David repeatedly from enemies within (his moral failures), and without (betrayal and violence) throughout his life.

Similarly, Stephen, a Holy Spirit-filled deacon in the early church, committed his spirit into God's care as he endured stoning by the religious zealots of his day. Luke gives us the story in the book of Acts:

> *"But they cried out with a loud voice and stopped their ears and rushed together at him. Then they cast him out of the city and stoned him. And the witnesses laid down their garments at the feet of a young man named Saul. And as they were stoning Stephen, he called out, "Lord Jesus, receive my spirit." Acts 7:57-59*

The cross of Jesus Christ is where Jesus died as our Substitute, and where we learn how to live and die to the glory of God. As we put our trust in God, realizing that He works all things together for our good (Romans 8:28), and we entrust our spirit into His hands, we have confidence that He will save us from all our distresses in life and death. As we do this, we are kept in perfect peace (Philippians 4:7) so that we can say with Paul, *"The Lord will rescue me from every evil deed and bring me safely into his heavenly kingdom. To Him, be the glory forever and ever. Amen." 2 Timothy 4:18*

Question 6. How does Jesus' final cry on the cross, *"Father, into Your hands, I commit my Spirit!"* teach you how to handle difficulties, hardships, trials and even death?

_____

_____

_____

_____

Ivy writes, *"This lesson has been very timely for me as I have recently had a biopsy to see if I have cancer. I can willingly commit my life to God, knowing that whatever He wants will be the absolute best for me. I'm loved with an everlasting love."*

Question 7. What has focusing on the cross in this lesson taught you, or brought to your remembrance?

_____

_____

_____

_____

Kristi writes, *"I am reminded of some really difficult times in my life, such as the death of each of my parents, and my husband losing his job at the age of 59 and being out of work for 14 months. I was able to come through these circumstances much easier when I surrendered the outcomes to God. I've, for the most part, learned to do this right away instead of agonizing over it. To me, surrender equals peace!"*

We have come to the end of our study, but certainly not to the end of our pursuit of finding life in Jesus' death. Friend, as long as we live on the earth, we must *"carry around in our body the death of Jesus so that the life of Jesus may also be revealed"* in us (2 Corinthians 4:10). May God enable you to focus on and apply the cross of Christ, receiving all its benefits in your life, for His glory and your good!

www.ingramcontent.com/pod-product-compliance
Lightning Source LLC
La Vergne TN
LVHW061222060426
835509LV00012B/1385